Ludicrous Laws and Mindless Misdemeanors

Lance S. Davidson

John Wiley & Sons, Inc.
New York • Chichester • Weinheim •
Brisbane • Singapore • Toronto

This publication is designed to provide accurate and authoritative
information in regard to the subject matter covered. It is sold with
the understanding that the publisher is not engaged in rendering
professional services. If legal, accounting, medical, psychological, or
any other expert assistance is required, the services of a competent
professional person should be sought.

ISBN 0-471-13897-5 (paper : alk. paper)

Printed in the United States of America
10 9 8 7 6 5 4 3 2 1

Ludicrous
Laws
and
Mindless
Misdemeanors

Contents

Introduction   vii

1   Food and Drink   1

2   Pets and Animals   11

3   Politics, Patriotism, and Religion   23

4   Sports and Games   35

5   Health and Safety   43

6   Sex   57

7   Trains, Cars, and Wacky Drivers   65

8   Crimes and Criminals   73

9   Grab Bag of More Weird Laws   85

10 Media and Pop Culture   93

11 Courtship, Marriage, and Divorce   105

12 Taxes and Big Business   115

13 Prison and Punishment   127

14 Wills   137

15 Lawyers   159

16 Judges   179

17 Poetic Justice   199

18 Just Plain Silly   211

19 Mixed Bag   221

Sources   229

Index of Names   239

Introduction

I've always been fascinated by wacky behavior, and by the even wackier cases and laws issued to protect the rest of us from ourselves. So I went to law school to satisfy the former craving and began to collect examples of legal absurdities to satisfy the latter. I've collected the best material to share here with you. You'll find actual laws, judgments, anecdotes, and quotations that demonstrate how truth really is stranger than fiction.

Perhaps it's my suspicious nature or training as an attorney, but when I read a book about outrageous cases or laws in which no citations appear, I wonder if the laws are true. The ones that make me most suspicious are the laws that are attributed to one state in one book, but to another state in another book. So to show that these unbelievable examples are, in fact, law, I have shown you where you can find each one, if you are so inclined.

But why have such laws been created when they are clearly ridiculous? There are a few reasons. One is that a legislator on occasion will include an absurd amendment to a bill in order to defeat the bill, and then, when the bill is passed, the bizarre law springs to life. Others are simply from a bygone era but were never officially taken off the books. Still others simply show that many of us never tire of trying to overrule human nature!

Although there is nothing logical about the laws in this book, I have attempted to organize its chapters into logical categories. We will cover many aspects of legal rules, including marriage and divorce, taxes, sports, health, cars and drivers, pop culture, sex, big business, and the like. At the end of the book are rules that are just plain silly—and those that truly defy categorization.

I would like to thank the following for their support: my parents, my wife and daughter, Tamara and Rachel, for constantly refreshing my sense of humor; Judith McCarthy and her colleagues at John Wiley & Sons for believing in this project and editing the manuscript; and my agent Sheree Bykofsky and her assistant, Janet Rosen, for their invaluable assistance.

And for the reader, enjoy! I am always on the lookout for wacky cases, laws, stories, and observations. Please send in additional material, with citations, to me care of my agent at: Sheree Bykofsky Associates, 11 East 47th Street, New York, NY 10017.

How the Laws and Court Decisions Are Cited

A few words about how the laws here are denoted might be in order to help you understand the book better. Like their more sensible counterparts, ludicrous laws (known as statutes when they are state laws) are often divided into chapters, which you'll see listed in "Chap." or sections, which you'll see denoted with the symbol "§." The appropriate state is also given for each.

As for court cases, there are official reports for decisions of the United States Supreme Court, but no official ones for the decisions of the United States Court of Appeals of the thirteen United States District Courts (consisting of 11 "Circuits" that cover several states each as listed below, one District of Columbia Circuit, and one Federal Circuit). These appear in unauthorized form in the *Federal Reporter* and the *Federal Supplement*. A citation for a U.S. Supreme Court decision would appear as, say, 600 U.S. 250 (1998), where "600" refers to the volume and "250" refers to the page of the reported decision. A "v." in the case name denotes "versus." A citation to a *Federal Reporter* would have an "F." or "F.2d" between the volume and page; a citation to a *Federal*

Supplement should have an "F.Supp." between volume and page. There are also seven reporters for the decisions of the intermediate appellate and highest court of each state. These are designated as follows: the *Northeastern* (N.E.), the *Northwestern* (N.W.), the *Atlantic* (A.), the *Southern* (S.), the *Southwestern* (S.W.), the *Southeastern* (S.E.), and the *Pacific* (P.). The *California Reporter* (Cal.Rptr.) and the *New York Supplement* (N.Y.S.)—which bring new meaning to the word "voluminous," with one ready to embark on to its fourth series—are additional reporters published for these two most litigious states.

That covers most of the citations you'll see, but like many of the laws themselves, the reporting system is a convoluted, irregular creature, so you may see some additional abbreviations, codes, or numbers.

Territory Covered by Each of the Eleven Circuit Courts

First Circuit Court	Second Circuit Court	Third Circuit Court
Maine	Connecticut	Delaware
Massachusetts	New York	New Jersey
New Hampshire	Vermont	Pennsylvania
Puerto Rico		U.S. Virgin Islands
Rhode Island		

**Fourth
Circuit Court**
North Carolina
South Carolina
Virginia
West Virginia

**Fifth
Circuit Court**
Louisiana
Mississippi
Texas

**Sixth
Circuit Court**
Kentucky
Michigan
Ohio
Tennessee

**Seventh
Circuit Court**
Illinois
Indiana
Wisconsin

**Eighth
Circuit Court**
Arkansas
Iowa
Minnesota
Missouri
Nebraska
North Dakota
South Dakota

**Ninth
Circuit Court**
Alaska
Arizona
California
Guam
Hawaii
Idaho
Montana
Nevada
Northern Mariana
 Islands
Oregon
Washington

**Tenth
Circuit Court**
Colorado
Kansas
New Mexico
Oklahoma
Utah

**Eleventh
Circuit Court**
Alabama
Florida
Georgia

◆ 1 ◆

Food
and
Drink

ountless laws govern what, when, and where we may eat and drink. The laws about alcohol are different in various parts of the country, ranging from few restrictions to almost complete restriction. Many of the laws about drinking are holdovers from the days of Prohibition, when the country as a whole decided to provide adult child-care for its inhabitants by prohibiting them from the use and abuse of alcohol. In the process, of course, Prohibition gave the biggest boost to organized crime ever known in this country's history.

Certainly there are good reasons for government regulations about the health and safety of food preparation and serving. But as you will see here, sometimes these laws are just plain silly.

——✦ Food for Thought ✦——

Arizona has legislated a "veggie hate crimes act." Farmers and shippers in that state can sue anyone who maliciously spreads false information about Arizona farm products.

—*Arizona Revised Statutes, §3-113*

✦

In Louisiana there are two kinds of fruit, but only one is "natural."

—*Louisiana Civil Code, §551*

✦

San Anselmo, California, banned the sale of candy called "cola sticks," as they "have the peculiar and singular characteristic of forming a black and sticky mass of pernicious quality."

Oddly, there are no laws about toupées.

—*San Anselmo (California) City Code, §S-7.02*

✦

In New Mexico it is a misdemeanor to sell imitation honey even if it is clearly labeled "imitation honey."

—*New Mexico Statutes, §25-9-3*

✦

There's no free lunch in Maryland—literally. Except for hors d'oeuvres, bars in that state cannot offer food for free.

—*Code of Maryland, §12-106*

✦

In Vermont it's illegal for vagrants to procure food by force. Does that mean if you have a good job and stable home life . . . then it's legal?

—*Vermont Statutes, §13-3906*

✦

In Tennessee you cannot throw a banana on the sidewalk. That must explain why no comedians were born there.

—*Tennessee Code, §39-17-307*

✦

The legislators in Wisconsin have declared that you need a license there to make cheese.

—*Wisconsin Statutes, §97.17*

✦

In New Jersey a license is required if you're in business to "break eggs" for any purpose.

—*New Jersey Statutes, §24:11-1*

✦

In San Francisco, County Supervisor Dan White was sore as hell that he had lost his job. In 1978 he went on a shooting rampage at City Hall, killing Mayor George Moscone and fellow San Francisco County Supervisor Harvey Milk. Charged with first-degree murder for the premeditated shootings, White pled temporary insanity. As part of his defense, White made the novel contention that the physiological effects of sugar and other ingredients in processed foods had rendered him unable to distinguish right from wrong.

The "Twinkie Defense" was successful and the court lessened the penalty to second-degree murder.

—People v. White, *City and County of San Francisco Sup. Ct. No. 98663 (1979)*

✦

A more sane approach to eating was taken by judges over a century ago in Georgia. During a trial a bailiff took the jury to lunch at a hotel kept by counsel for the party that later prevailed. It didn't appear that other accommodations were available. In rejecting the loser's contention of prejudice, the court remarked, "In this degenerate age, jurors must eat."

—Brinson v. Faircloth,
82 Georgia 185, 7 S.E. 923 (1888)

✦

Yet even over a hundred years ago, jurists understood that nourishment did have its limits. In 1874 the mountaineer Alferd Packer, guiding five homesteaders along the Mormon Trail into Colorado during a stormy winter, emerged alone from the San Juan Mountains. The amazing truth soon emerged—Packer had eaten all five men. When sentencing Packer to hang for cannibalism, Judge Melville B. Gerry reportedly shouted, "Stand up, yah voracious man-eatin' sonofabitch and receive your sintince! Thar were only sivin Dimocrats in all of Hinsdale County 'n' ya et five o' thim!"

(In tribute, the cafeteria at the University of Colorado at Boulder is known as the Alferd G. Packer Grill.)

—Oliver D. Loutsenhiser, Packer's Cannibalism *(1887)*

—✦Constricting Commerce✦—

There's one less job opportunity in Maryland than in other states. Female "sitters" or "shills," used by tavern owners to lure male patrons to buy drinks, are outlawed.

—Code of Maryland, §27-152

✦

Denial of equal protection? It is illegal in Nebraska to sell liquor to people in their motor vehicles, unless they are handicapped.

—Revised Statutes of Nebraska, §53-178.01

✦

It is now, finally, legal to sell alcoholic beverages in nudist colonies in California.

—*California Business and Professions Code, §25750*

✦

Drinking booze is forbidden at tailgate parties outside sports stadiums in Maryland. But during the game you may buy booze *in* the stadium.

—*Code of Maryland, §19-202*

✦

In Utah, anyone who is drunk cannot legally purchase a drink. But if you're really drunk, howya gonna know that you're really drunk?

—*Utah Code, §32A-12-210*

Michigan's state legislature took action to declare that using pictures of deceased United States presidents to sell liquor is illegal. (Next, they'll outlaw using deceased future presidents.)

—Michigan Compiled Laws, §750.42

✦

In Tempe, Arizona, you may drink booze in a city park only if it is larger than three acres.

—Tempe (Arizona) City Code, §637.7

2

Pets and Animals

A dog is man's best friend, or so the saying goes. So it's a good thing dogs—and cats, ferrets, horses, hamsters, parrots, and chickens, for that matter—can't read. If they could, they would know about all the laws regulating their behavior, and they might start really misbehaving to justify enactment of the laws! Worse, they might find someone else to befriend.

✦ Animal Animus ✦

A burglar had stolen a stretched bear-hide from the living room wall of a homeowner named Starry. When Starry submitted a claim to his insurance company, the insurer denied coverage. Horace Mann Insurance Company asserted that the policy exclusion for "furs" excluded the hide from coverage. Under two subheads in his opinion, "Bear Facts" and "Bear Coverage," the judge wrote:

A burglar, as it were, left the wall
bare, as it wasn't. . . . Horace Mann,
baring claws of its own, invoked the
policy's exclusionary clause.

Judge Compton held the insurer liable.
—Starry v. Horace Mann Ins. Co.,
649 P.2d 937 (Alaska 1982)

✦

In Great Britain, a "tame" circus elephant named Buffa was snapped at by the
plaintiff's dog, which was not authorized to be
on the premises. The elephant, chasing the dog,
knocked over a stall, thereby seriously injuring
a midget. The defendant argued that his elephant was not of a savage disposition, and
therefore shouldn't come under the strict liability rule of injury from a *ferae naurae* (wild
animal). The court held, as a matter of law, that
all elephants are dangerous.

Observed Lord Devlin, "If a person wakes
up in the middle of the night and finds an
escaping tiger on top of his bed and suffers a
heart attack, it would be nothing to the point
that the intentions of the tiger were quite
amiable."
—Behrens v. Bertram Mills Circus Ltd.,
2 Kings Bench, England, 1 (1957)

✦

Although little could be more prosaic than a dog soiling a rug, one man sued his neighbor for the affront. Mr. Kaufman's attorney alleged that "whenever [the defendant Vosmik's cocker spaniel] felt the pressure of certain natural urgings, he (she) was inclined to favor with these indelicate attentions the soft and absorbent spaces of plaintiff's lovely carpeting." Because of this Kaufman sought $300 and the costs of the lawsuit "and any other doggone rights to which the court feels he is entitled." Not to be outdone, the defendant's counsel answered in doggerel, and even the judge joined in the merriment:

> The Court has heard the defendant's tale
> And listened to the plaintiff's wail.
> Methinks the dog that Joe doth own
> Does more than gnaw upon its bone.
> The rug by drink its fate did seal
> But will outlast the dead "New Deal."
> So Joe pay Joe and let's play ball.
> Dismissed and settled, once for all.
>
> —Kaufman v. Vosmik,
> *Case no. 848941 (Cleveland Muni. Ct. 1937)*

✦

Do the rules of self-defense govern a dogfight, a real one? One nineteenth-century New York case concerned a dogfight in which the plaintiff alleged that the defendant had set his dog upon the plaintiff's dog or, in the alternative, knew of his dog's vicious propensities. The plaintiff's dog died from the injuries it incurred in the dogfight.

Judge Allen wrote that settling a dogfight between dogs instead of their masters was a case of first impression, despite having presided over other cases in which the masters of dogs had

> acquitted themselves in a manner which might well have aroused the envy of their canine dependents. . . . I am constrained to admit total ignorance of the code *duello* among dogs, or what constitutes a just cause of offense and justifies a resort to the *ultima ratio regem*, a resort to arms, or rather to teeth, for redress. . . . It is not claimed, upon either side, that the struggle was not in all respects doglike and fair. . . .

Judge Allen went on to observe that he was not aware that dogs had to resort to legal tomes to resolve their differences. Nonetheless, he found that the laws of nature superseded those of mankind, and denied the plaintiff recovery.

—*Wiley v. Slater,*
22 Barb. 506 (New York App.Div. 1856)

✦

And while we're on pets . . . The owner of Blackie the Talking Cat sued when the city of Augusta, Georgia, demanded a license tax in order for him to exhibit his cat, which he had allegedly taught to speak a few words. The appeals court cleverly sprinkled "cat" into words throughout the opinion—catechism, catapulted, catalyst, cataclysmic, category, and catatonic. Even the free speech rights of a cat who had told a federal judge "I love you" were discussed.

The court then declined to permit Blackie's owner to argue on the cat's behalf that its right to free speech had been infringed: "Blackie can clearly speak for himself." Blackie didn't, and lost the case.

—*Miles v. City Council of Augusta,*
710 F.2d 1542 (11th Cir. 1983)

✦

The dogged ability of a federal officer to ferret out evidence against the defendant was important in a drug-trafficking case. The case turned on whether seized evidence that could implicate the defendant would be admissible as evidence. In the absence of a search warrant, a reasonable belief of criminal activity is required for a search and seizure by government agents. The federal officer claimed that he could smell marijuana as well as a dog, and became reasonably suspicious:

> The ubiquitous DEA agent Paul Markonni once again sticks his nose into the drug trade. This time he is on the scent of appellant Mitchell Sentovich's drug courier activities. We now learn that among Markonni's many talents is an olfactory sense we in the past attributed only to canines. Sentovich argues that he should have been able to test . . . whether Markonni is really the human bloodhound he claims to be. Sentovich's claims, however, have more bark than bite. In fact, they have not a dog's chance of success.
>
> —United States v. Sentovich,
> *677 F.2d 834 (11th Cir. 1982)*

✦

There's another reason to observe the "leash law" in Tennessee. There, anyone, without liability, may cripple or even kill a "proud bitch" running at large.

—*Tennessee Code, §44-8-411*

✦ Agrarian Culture ✦

It's getting tougher to break into show biz. In California, a nonresident pig must get a note from its doctor before going on stage; just its exhibition requires a health certificate.

—*California Food and Agriculture Code, §10721*

✦

County commissioners in Nevada may outlaw livestock on a highway so long as the highway is fenced on both sides.

—*Nevada Revised Statutes, §244.355*

✦

It is illegal in California for you to possess more than one bear gallbladder.

—*California Fish and Game Code, §4758*

✦

Dumbo can rest easy. In California, it is illegal to abuse an elephant.

—*California Penal Code, §596.5*

✦

In California, a bull will never be lonely. He is required by law to be in the company of at least thirty cows while grazing in the open range.

—*California Food and Agriculture Code, §16233*

✦

Theft or poaching of a bear or deer in New Hampshire is illegal, but only if you're a "natural person."

—*New Hampshire Revised Statutes, §208: 9-A*

✦

During Idaho's fall and winter, livestock may not graze within the boundaries of cities containing over five hundred inhabitants. If unattended.

—*Idaho Code, §25-2112*

✦

Unless they are within 400 feet of town limits, and the inhabitants have an unobstructed view, horses and donkeys in California may perform the physical act of love *alfresco*.

—*California Food and Agriculture Code, §16701*

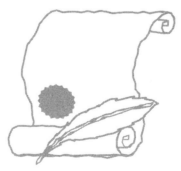

⬥The Racing Game⬥

A plaintiff was awarded nearly $200,000 for the defendant's failure to promote an Arabian colt named Score. The award was in spite of the fact that the colt died before the date when the defendant was to begin marketing the colt. The court of appeals, affirming the lower court's judgment, began its opinion:

> Beating dead horses is the sport of appellate judges, a generally harmless pasttime painful only to the readers of appellate opinions. Paying for the promotion of dead horses can be an expensive proposition, however, as the facts of this case make abundantly clear.
>
> —Arabian Score v. Lasma Arabian Ltd.,
> *814 F.2d 529 (8th Cir. 1987)*

⬥

In Arizona, a "horse" can also be an ass, a mule, or a burro.

—*Arizona Revised Statutes, §3-2121*

⬥

In case you're planning to, it's illegal in Connecticut, without government approval, to import horse semen.

—*Connecticut General Statutes, §22-415h*

3

Politics,
Patriotism,
and
Religion

Here in the land of the free one would assume the term "religious law" to be an oxymoron. But alas, it is not so.

Sunday is still the day of rest in New Jersey (and elsewhere), even though much of the rest of the country is shopping. The "blue laws" forbidding retail stores to open on Sundays have had Bergen County, New Jersey, retailers up in arms for years. And every year like clockwork newspapers report that parents want their children to be allowed to pray in school.

Separation of church and state? What's that?

──◆ Religious Ligature ◆──

By its Constitution, the state of Arkansas disqualifies an atheist from holding office or testifying as a witness.
>   —*Arkansas Constitution, Article 19, §1*

◆

In Kentucky, it is illegal to use reptiles during religious services.

—*Kentucky Revised Statutes, §437.060*

✦

Maine holds the Lord's day sacred, except when there is serious money to be made. There, it's illegal to keep a business open on Sunday—except during the Christmas shopping season.

—*Maine Revised Statutes, §17-3204*

✦

Are prayers to God capable of being intercepted by the government? In Canada, yes.

A suspected arsonist was arrested by the Royal Canadian Mounted Police. While awaiting a lie detector test, he slid out of his chair onto the ground. On his knees with his arms outstretched, the suspect begged, "Oh God, let me get away with it just once."

Unfortunately for him, the room was bugged and a videotape of his self-incriminating statement was offered into evidence at his trial. The defendant objected that the videotape violated a Canadian law that prohibited intercepting private communications if it was reasonable to expect that only the person intended to be called would receive the communication. The court agreed with the prosecutor's argument that God was not the kind of "person" contemplated by the law.

—Regina v. Davie,
*17 Canadian Reports, Third Series p. 72
(British Columbia Court of Appeal, Canada 1980)*

✦

The court system is pervasive in American life; no matter is too self-evident that doesn't deserve its day in court. The California appellate bench held in one case that a city may discharge a school bus driver who believes in the religious sacrifice of children.

—Hollon v. Pierce,
257 California App. 2d 468 (3d Dist. 1967)

✦The Fraud Squad ✦

Fraud has always been popular, but was especially so at the beginning of the twentieth century. An anecdote from that time has a judge, following sentencing, leaning over and asking the defendant, a swindler, "How could you cheat those people who so trusted you?"

"Judge," the con man explains, "you can't cheat people who *don't* trust you."

The story behind this? It turns out that an enterprising Texas realtor advertised a certain ranch property in various parts of the country and deceived many trusting members of the public. He described it as richer than the valleys of Southern California, said that it could not be kept from becoming a land of gold, that it was a land of fruit and flowers and happy homes, and that all eyes were on Texas, particularly Southwest Texas. He even added references to Aladdin's lamp and the Garden of Eden.

Though many a proud Texan would have argued otherwise, the Texas court held that the statements were too "extraordinary . . . to take them . . . at their face."

—Buckingham v. Thompson,
135 S.W. 652 (1911)

✦

In another case involving fraud, a Utopian group took up quarters in New Mexico and wrote its own bible and elected its own god. To increase its membership the Faithists distributed excerpts from their bible describing the land they inhabited (the Land of Shalam) and its environs: "Next south lay the kingdom of Himalawowoaganapapa . . . [and i]n the high north lay the kingdom of Olegalla, the land of giants, the place of yellow rocks and high spouting waters. Olegalla it was who gave away his kingdom, the great city of Powafuchwowitchavagganeabba, spread along the valley of Anemoosagoochakakfuela." (Observed the court, "This unquestionably refers to Chicago.")

The plaintiff, who had been with the group for over a year, contended that he had been defrauded by the Faithists into believing they had in fact found Utopia. The Faithists countered that the plaintiff could read maps to determine where he truly was and was of ordinary intelligence, which he admitted. Bad move. The court held that only if he were an imbecile could he claim to rely on such patently ridiculous material.

—Ellis v. Newbrough,
6 New Mexico 181, 27 P. 490 (1891)

——✦Impolitic Politics✦——

State law in Arkansas stipulates that you cannot hold office there within ten years of fighting a duel or even acting as a second or carrying a challenge.

> —*Arkansas Constitution, Article 19 §2*

✦

The Roman writer Juvenal posed the rhetorical question nearly two thousand years ago: "*Sed quis cusiodiet ipsos Custodes?*" (Who shall guard the guards themselves?) Delaware's legislature can amend the state constitution without voter approval.

> —*Delaware Constitution of 1897, Article XVI §1*

✦

In Kentucky, it's against the law for politicians to hand out alcoholic beverages on Election Day.

> —*Kentucky Revised Statutes, §119.215*

✦

Maine, a state of sparse population, requires nine people to sit on the Displaced Homemakers Advisory Council. The advisors may advise the advised where to place themselves.

—Maine Revised Statutes, 26 §1604

◆ Civic Pride ◆
and Prejudice

The final "s" in Arkansas is silent. It's the law.

—Arkansas Code of 1987, §1-4-105

◆

The only correct pronunciation of Joliet, Illinois, is Joliet, with the accent on the first syllable, and the "o" long.

—*City of Joliet (Illinois) Administration Code, §2-8*

◆

You can urinate, defecate, and vomit on the Confederate flag in Florida—unless it's for crass purposes.

—*Florida Statutes, §256.10*

◆

The legislative history of Arkansas's law against sodomy absolutely, positively leaves no doubt as to its interpretation. The bill, signed into law by the state's governor in 1977, was passed unanimously as "aimed at weirdos and queers who live in a fairyland world and are trying to wreck family life." Sex with one of the same gender could result in a fine or jail time, or both.

—*Arkansas Code of 1987, §5-14-122*

◆

San Francisco, as you might guess, has long enjoyed the trappings of a "police state." The police commission of that city may appoint private citizens as special patrol officers who then have a *proprietary interest* in their beat: The beat can be sold and may be bequeathed to heirs.

—*San Francisco (California) Charter,*
Chapter 33, §3.536

✦

It is illegal in Michigan to be caught playing "The Star Spangled Banner" for dancing. Here's one case where an insanity plea will work every time as a defense.

—*Michigan Compiled Laws, §750.542*

✦

"A Constitution should be short and obscure."

—*Napoleon I (Napoleon Bonaparte) (1769–1821),*
French general and emperor, Maxims (1804–1815)

✦

"No matter whether th' constitution follows th' flag or not, th' supreme coort follows th' iliction returns."

—*Finley Peter Dunne (1867–1936),
American writer and humorist*, Mr. Dooley's
Opinions 'The Supreme Court's Decisions' *(1901)*

◆ Lawlessness ◆

"Now this is the Law of the Jungle—as old and as true as the sky."

—*Rudyard Kipling (1865–1936),
English writer and poet,*
Second Jungle Book, 'The Law of the Jungle' *(1895)*

◆

"Here, even the law of the jungle has broken down."

—*Walid Jumblatt (1949–   ), Lebanese militant,
describing the civil war in Lebanon, quoted in*
Sunday Times *(London, December 29, 1985)*

◆

"Wherever Law ends, Tyranny begins."

—*John Locke (1632–1704), English philosopher,* Second Treatise of Government, Sec. 202 *(1690)*

◆

"Take but degree away, untune that string,
And, hark! what discord follows."

—*William Shakespeare (1564–1616), English playwright and poet,* Troilus and Cressida *(1603)*

◆

"Anarchism is a game at which the police can beat you."

—*George Bernard Shaw (1856–1950), Irish playwright,* Misalliance *(1914)*

4

Sports and Games

Once upon a time, say a hundred years ago, this country's population was smaller by many millions, and its open space vaster by thousands of square miles. People carried guns and used them regularly. And the words "gun" and "sport" had nothing in common.

Today it's not unreasonable to expect laws governing the use of firearms. Yes, the Bill of Rights assures us of the freedom to bear arms, but these days most people expect some restrictions on where and when we may do so. We need laws that differentiate between killing a predatory animal and killing a neighbor because his boom box is too loud.

What's surprising are some of the other ways lawmakers have seen fit to legislate leisure-time activities, from fishing to gambling. Here are some of the strangest.

✦ Ain't Misbehavin' ✦

A boys' stickball game erupted into a fight between a 127-pound plaintiff and a 220-pound defendant, who had verbally challenged the plaintiff. The court, in awarding $150 to the young plaintiff in a directed verdict, wrote:

> The plaintiff hero . . . scornful of the fact that a "soft answer turneth away wrath," retorted in what in the lexicon of youth is called "a snappy comeback: "Do you think you're big enough?" . . . Whatever plaintiff's doubts may have been expressed by his query, they were immediately resolved by the action of the [defendant]. . . . The plaintiff's injuries were diagnosed as a fractured jaw, for which injury he now seeks a poultice of damages. [The plaintiff's pugnacity and provocation] does not excuse the defendant for "slapping the plaintiff down" as he might a troublesome mosquito. . . . Let the plaintiff learn to keep his tongue in his cheek and the defendant his hands in his pockets.

—Henderson v. Weiss, *Supreme Court of New York, Trial Term (1935)*

✦

In Nevada, boxing and wrestling competitions in which a punch is not reasonably expected to inflict injury are not subject to laws regulating "unarmed combat." Well, at least that eliminates *professional* boxing and wrestling.

—*Nevada Revised Statutes, §467.0107*

✦

If you still have lingering doubts about your golf swing, scratch one concern if you play in Massachusetts. It's illegal there to manufacture, sell, or knowingly use an exploding golf ball.

—*Massachusetts General Laws, Chapter 148, §55*

✦

A bowling alley—but not a dance hall or a pool hall—set up next door to a school or church is subject to a daily fine in Vermont.

—*Vermont Statutes, §31-509*

✦

To be exempt from waterway tolls, Louisiana, doing its part to fight pollution, requires pleasure boats to be powered by internal combustion engines.

—*Louisiana Revised Statutes, 34 §831*

✦

If you're in a rush, fish in Washington. True, it's illegal to catch fish by throwing rocks at them, but explosives aren't prohibited.

—*Revised Code of Washington, §75.12.070*

✦

In Maine, it's illegal to catch lobster with your bare hands.

—*Maine Revised Statutes, §6432*

✦

It's becoming harder to hunt in Colorado. Hunters there can no longer hunt ducks from an airplane.

—*Colorado Revised Statutes, §33-6-124*

✦

It requires a state license to gather alligator eggs in Florida (not to mention a certain amount of nerve).

—*Florida Statutes, §372.663*

—✦ Fraught with Fraud ✦—

Fake professional wrestling is barred in Washington. Still looking for the real thing.

> —*Revised Code of Washington, §67.08.110*

✦

The gambling capital of the world, Nevada, describes every game imaginable for its defining legislation of gambling except "spin the bottle."

> —*Nevada Revised Statutes, §463.0152*

—✦ But It's Not My Fault ✦—

"Heads I win, tails you lose." When Leonard Tose, ex-owner of the Philadelphia Eagles football team, lost $1.2 million gambling at the Sands Casino and Hotel in Atlantic City, the casino sued him for his gambling debts. Tose counterclaimed to recover his losses, claiming that the casino should be held liable for allowing him to gamble while he was drunk.

Though a judge affirmed his right to sue, Tose lost his audacious lawsuit.

> —*Tose v. Greate Bay Hotel and Casino,*
> *819 F. Supp. 1312 (D. New Jersey 1993)*

✦ Decreeing ✦ Good Manners

"Fair is foul, and foul is fair." How often does a backyard game of hoops erupt into a lawsuit? Well, one defendant wound up in court for bad manners. Two neighbors—*both* lawyers—represented themselves against each other.

The sound of the Schild family playing basketball so infuriated Rubin that he sprayed the Schilds and their basketball court with a garden hose. Both men sued for various misdeeds and to obtain injunctions against the other. The action quickly rose from little league playing to major league bickering. Featured at one of Rubin's hearings was scientific testimony by acoustical engineers, architects, and real estate appraisers.

The courts found neither willful harassment by Schild nor emotional distress by Rubin—except that "generated by the litigation in this case." So much for home court advantage.

—Schild v. Rubin,
233 Cal.App.3d 755 (California Ct.App. 1991)

✦

If someone doesn't accept a challenge to duel in Michigan, it's a misdemeanor for you to scoff at him in a poster.

—*Michigan Compiled Laws, §750.173*

✦

Like most states, Arizona forbids dueling. But it doesn't stop there. You'd also be in violation of the law if you know of a dueling challenge and don't report it, even if the challenge hasn't been sent. Not surprisingly, no would-be duellists have 'fessed up in order to serve time.

—*Arizona Revised Statutes, §26-1114*

✦

In Washington you cannot ride a bike unless using the "permanent and regular seat." No riding the seat column.

—*Revised Code of Washington, §46.61.760*

✦

In a laudatory effort to improve air quality, Springfield, Illinois, prohibits commercial establishments from permitting or promoting dwarf-tossing.

—*City of Springfield, Illinois, Code of Ordinances, §90.61*

✦

5

Health
and
Safety

Used to be that if you tripped over your own two feet as you were walking across the street, you were assumed to be clumsy and cautioned to be more careful. That would be that.

Nowadays, you'd be advised to sue the asphalt maker who poured the tar, the town that decided to build the road, the planner who drew the specifications, and perhaps even the Department of Transportation on general principles.

Megabuck lawsuits are in the news these days, that's for sure. Whatever your opinion on this controversial topic, you'd do well to read this chapter. You'll learn about some of the hapless people who sued—and lost.

—✦ Someone Always Loses ✦—

After winning a $2 million settlement in 1991 for injuries she claimed she suffered at a restaurant, Annie Marie Leal rose out of her wheelchair and walked—in high heels. That was a costly mistake: Steak & Ale, the restaurant chain, had it on videotape.

Back in 1989, a waiter had dropped a tray full of dinners on Ms. Leal. She sued, blaming the Texas-size steaks for causing her Texas-size head, neck, and back injuries. The restaurant made an offer of settlement; she agreed; and the judge approved it orally but hadn't yet signed the judgment.

Then Ms. Leal, who had attended much of her trial in a wheelchair, was spotted walking unaided and driving an unmodified vehicle, contrary to testimony. Steak & Ale sought to void the settlement agreement and, finally, in 1995, the Texas Supreme Court threw it out because it hadn't been signed by the trial judge.

Next time, Leal should eat takeout.

—S & A Restaurant Corp. v. Leal,
38 Texas Sup. Ct. J. 303, 892 S.W.2d 855 (1995)

✦

A young man claiming damages for an arm injury caused by a bus driver's negligence was being cross-examined by British barrister (and later member of Parliament) F. E. Smith, Lord Birkenhead. Birkenhead said, "Please show us how high you can lift your arm now." The plaintiff, his face distorted in pain, slowly raised his arm to shoulder level.

"Thank you," said Birkenhead. "And now, please show us how high you could lift it before the accident." The arm quickly shot straight up in the air.

Birkenhead's client won the case.

—*Frederick Edwin Smith, 1st Earl of Birkenhead*
(1872–1930), British lawyer and politician;
Harriet Martineau, Autobiography, *reported in*
John Sutherland, ed., The Oxford Book of
Literary Anecdotes *(1975)*

✦

In Iowa, the Supreme Court ruled that a physician is entitled to recover for his services even though he was mistaken in his treatment.

—Whitesell v. Hill,
101 Iowa 629, 70 N.W. 750 (1897)

✦

Homeowners in Marin County, California, sacrifice their privacy to live there. They must admit, with a warrant or not, a county health inspector to their home during business hours.

—*Marin County (California) Ordinance, 141 §2*

✦

In skydiving, it's not the fall you should be afraid of, but of hitting the ground. Victims in slip-and-fall cases discover gravity the hard way, too. A couple was dancing at a catered wedding banquet before slipping and falling. Asparagus spears, covered with sauce from the tray of a waiter as he negotiated through the crowded dance floor, were also grounded.

First.

The couple sued. With wry sarcasm, Justice Michael A. Musmanno of Pennsylvania observed:

> It can be stated as an incontrovertible legal proposition that anyone attending a dinner dance has the inalienable right to expect that, if asparagus is to be served, it will be served on the dinner table and not on the dance floor.

The couple won the suit for damages against the hotel due to negligence.

—Schwartz v. Warwick-Philadelphia Corp.,
424 Pennsylvania 185, 226 A.2d 484 (1967)

✦

Like the preternatural bickering between dogs and cats, lawyers and physicians have squared off repeatedly to trade verbal jabs at each other. When asked to identify himself, a witness in a case pompously declared, "I employ myself as a surgeon."

Demanded Baron Edward Law Ellenborough, "But does anyone else employ you as a surgeon?"

—*Edward Law Ellenborough, 1st Baron (1750–1818), British lawyer and jurist, reported in W. Davenport Adams,* The Treasury of Modern Anecdotes *(1886)*

✦

A prisoner named Ned Searight had claimed $12 million damages for being taken, while in custody, to Newark's Eye, Ear and Speech Clinic. There, he charged, the state had him injected in the left eye with a radium electric beam and, as a result, someone talked to him on the inside of his brain. The judge found his complaint groundless, writing:

The allegations, of course, are of facts which, if they exist, are not yet known to man. . . . [Even] Mr. Houdini has so far failed to establish communication from the spirit world. . . . But, taking the facts as pleaded, and assuming them to be true, they show a case of presumably unlicensed radio communication, a matter which comes within the sole jurisdiction of the Federal Communications Commission [citation]. And even aside from that, Searight could have blocked the broadcast to the antenna in his brain simply by grounding it . . . [and] pinned to the back of a trouser leg a short chain of paper clips so that the end would touch the ground and prevent anyone from talking to him inside his brain.

—Searight v. New Jersey,
412 F.Supp. 413 (D. New Jersey 1976)

Then there's the case of the burglar who fortuitously won a lifetime annuity just because he fell through a skylight and became paralyzed. As a prank, teenager Rick Bodine and some friends attempted to remove a floodlight from the roof of a school in order to light a tennis court. Bodine fell through a skylight that had been painted the same color as the roof. His injuries left him brain damaged, a quadriplegic, and unable to speak.

The school district was aware of the roof's dangerous condition because someone had already died at another school in the district after falling through a similarly camouflaged skylight. Three days into the trial, the school's insurer decided to settle.

—Bodine v. Enterprise High School,
CV 73225 (Shasta Co. Super. Ct., California 1982)

✦

After leaving a party an intoxicated Sang Yeul Lee felt the urge to relieve himself. He couldn't read English, so signs posted "Danger," "Electric Current," and "Keep Out" did not deter him. Nor was Lee deterred by a row of uneven boards laid out to ward off trespassers; he staggered across them, and then urinated.

He had quite a shock. Lee, having relieved himself on the Chicago Transit Authority's third line, which carried 600 volts of electricity, was zapped dead. His family sued for negligence and the Illinois Supreme Court affirmed the jury verdict of $1.5 million. Although the CTA had posted warnings, and Lee was drunk and trespassing, the decision required that the CTA devise a way to protect drunks from being electrocuted when they urinate on its tracks.

—Lee v. Chicago Transit Authority,
152 Illinois 2d 432, 605 N.E.2d 493 (1992)

✦

In one case, the plaintiffs were physicians who sought a temporary restraining order to prevent the Secretary of Health and Human Services from carrying out a plan to recover Medicare overpayments. The opinion was divided into the following headings:

PATIENT'S MEDICAL HISTORY

SYMPTOMS

TAKE TWO ASPIRIN AND CALL ME IN THE MORNING

CURING THE ILLNESS BUT LOSING THE PATIENT?

SEEKING A SECOND OPINION

CAN WE EASE THE PAIN?

—Texas Medical Ass'n. v. Sullivan,
875 F.2d 1160 (5th Cir. 1989)

—✦It's for Your Own Good ✦—

The state of South Carolina found it necessary to pass a law stating that you can't crawl around the public sewer system unless you have a permit.

—*Code of Laws of South Carolina, §5-31-20*

✦

In Vermont, where people walk on water, one is subject to a penalty if he draws ice from the water and fails to fence the hole. There are many holes in the water in Vermont.

—*Vermont Statutes, §13-3831*

✦

It is unlawful to put your hand near a container in North Carolina if you know it contains a venomous reptile.

—*North Carolina General Statutes, §14-418*

✦

If you plan to pile any lumber in Marin County, California, you should know that the law requires at least two feet of open air underneath the pile. Perhaps levitating lumber is sold there too.

—*Marin County (California) Ordinance, 141 §8*

✦

In Vermont, anyone (including a child) possessing a slingshot with the intent of using it can be imprisoned and fined.

—Vermont Statutes, §13-4001

✦

To get paid for braiding hair in Florida, you must learn about communicable diseases such as HIV/AIDS.

—Florida Statutes, §477.0132

✦

"*[L]a majestueuse égalité des lois, qui interdit au riche comme au pauvre de coucher sous les ponts, de mendier dans les rues et de voler du pain.*" (The law, in its majestic equality, forbids the rich as well as the poor to sleep under bridges, to beg in the streets, and to steal bread.)

—Anatole France (Jacques-Anatole-François Thibault), 1844–1924, French writer and poet,
Le Lys Rouge (The Red Lily) *(1894)*

✦ Emotionally ✦ Distressing

The justices of Virginia's Supreme Court found that 340 "hang-up" calls over a period of two months to a single mother were not unreasonably distressful.

—Russo v. White,
241 Virginia 23, 400 S.E.2d 160 (1991)

✦

It was the kind of hospital that, in the best Orwellian doublespeak, would tell you, "You are receiving adequate care because this is the best care the hospital can give you."

A new mother successfully sued a Tennessee hospital for severe emotional distress when her infant died soon after birth and was displayed to her in a jar of formaldehyde. The hospital and its counsel had refused to settle and allowed this case to reach the courts. After winning a big settlement, an attorney for the plaintiff was buckling up his briefcase. The insurance company representative angrily said to him, "I look forward to the day when I can write a check to your widow."

—Johnson v. Woman's Hospital,
527 S.W.2d 133 (Tennessee Ct.App. 1975)

✦

A fable handed down over the years among judges concerns the wise advice a retiring judge gave to a newly appointed one: "The most important aspect to being a good judge is sincerity. Once you learn how to fake it, you've got it made. If you're lucky, you'll get that dour judicial countenance that only a bad case of hemorrhoids can accomplish."

A judicial effort to mask callousness with an air of compassion was transparent in an Oregon case; even by the standards of the Depression, the judge's damages award was absurdly low. The award was upheld on appeal, but a lone dissenting judge put it succinctly: "$13.44 is not enough compensation for a broken neck."

—*Stacy v. State Industrial Accident Comm'n,*
145 Oregon 195, 26 P.2d 1092 (1933)

6

Sex

O tempora, O mores! Legislate sexual behavior? Perish the thought! Most people believe that what goes on behind closed doors in the privacy of their own homes is nobody's business but their own.

That may have been true once, when sex actually went on behind those aforementioned closed doors. But these days, sex is every-where—on billboards, in magazines, on TV, even on the sides of buses. So legislation is inevitable.

You might assume that the topics of sex and the courtroom would be mutually exclusive. Well, you'd be wrong, as this anecdote attests:

A sexual harassment victim tearfully tried to answer her lawyer as he probed her to testify on what the defendant had said to her before the alleged incident. "It's disgraceful how he propositioned me!" she cried. "I just can't bring myself to repeat his crude remarks."

Unable to evoke a response, the attorney scribbled on a notepad and handed it to her. "Was this what he said to you?" he asked.

The witness murmured, "Yes."

The attorney took back the note, and with the court's permission, circulated the note among the jury members. After her turn reading the note, one aghast young woman tried to pass the note. But the juror seated beside her was asleep so she elbowed him. Stirring, he took the note, slowly read it, winked at her, and slipped the note into his pocket before resuming his slumber.

✦

When twenty-nine-year-old Gloria Sykes hit her head and leg against the cable car she was riding in San Francisco in 1964, it appeared on first examination that she had merely suffered two leg bruises and a sprained neck. But later she discovered that the accident had caused her serious psychological and neurological trauma. Suddenly, she became a nymphomaniac and, as her suit alleged, she had engaged in sexual relations with over one hundred men as a consequence of her run-in with the cable car.

A doctor sarcastically testified for the defense that whatever problems she had experienced would be cured by a verdict. The jury, out nine hours, did not acquiesce to Ms. Sykes's demand for $500,000, but the court did award her $50,000 in damages.

—Sykes v. San Francisco,
No. 551479 (San Francisco, California Sup.Ct. 1970)

✦

Flushed with his success in the *Sykes* case, Ms. Sykes's attorney, Marvin Lewis, took on the case of a fifty-year-old mother of three from Santa Ana, California, who sued a health club for $1 million for traumatic neurosis. She charged that she had been trapped in a sweltering sauna for a substantial period of time (later established to be between three and eight minutes). The experience was so debilitating to her that, she claimed, she dislocated her jaw just from screaming for help.

As another consequence of her confinement, she was compelled to pick up twenty-four men in bars, despite being a devout Catholic and an attentive wife. The jury, out for two days following a three-and-one-half-month-long trial, did not award any damages.

—Parson v. Holiday Health Spa,
No. 173686 (Orange County, California Sup.Ct. 1974)

✦

Less sure of themselves were the justices of Oregon's Supreme Court in a recent case. A defendant challenged his conviction in Oregon for touching a woman's breasts without her consent by contending that he had not violated the relevant state statute. It prohibited touching another's "sexual or other intimate parts" without that person's consent, and he claimed that he had not touched "intimate parts."

The Oregon Supreme Court wouldn't touch that one. "Are lips intimate parts? Are knees or feet intimate, hands or elbows not?" The court determined that this was an issue to be decided by the jury in each case, so the conviction stood.

—State v. Woodley,
306 Oregon 458, 760 P.2d 884 (1988)

✦

Despite a dissenting justice's observation that "the real culprit was Osborn's endogenous salaciousness," Wyoming's Supreme Court revived Richard Osborn's lawsuit. So, instead of dismissing the case, his suit was sent back to the lower court to be heard. Osborn had claimed that he should be awarded more than $50,000 because an adult video was not X-rated enough.

According to Osborn, the star Busty Belle appeared for less than ten minutes in the video. As a result, Osborn sought $55.79 in medical costs for an asthma attack he claimed he suffered due to the "stress and strain of being ripped off," $50,000 for pain and suffering, $29.95 for the cost of the video, and punitive damages. (The trial court again dismissed the complaint, but this time the court's decision was affirmed on appeal.)

—*Osborn v. Emporium Videos,*
848 P.2d 237 (Wyoming 1993)

✦

In Nevada, where prostitution is legal, a "John" can sleep with a prostitute in a house of ill repute but he cannot *sleep* with her. Business is business.

—*Nevada Revised Statutes, §207.030*

✦ Forbidden Sex ✦

In South Carolina, fornication and adultery are punishable by fine and imprisonment. (Fornication is where neither partner is married; adultery is where one or both partners are married . . . but not to each other.)

—*Code of Laws of South Carolina, §16-15-60*

✦

In Washington State, you cannot molest your fishing gear. Ouch!

—*Revised Code of Washington, §75.12.090*

✦

For the truly creative sadomasochist, Minnesota's law against sodomy also prohibits sex between humans and birds.

—*Minnesota Statutes, §609.294*

✦

The Arizona legislature unintentionally (or intentionally) prohibited crimes against nature only with an adult. Apparently, however, it's legal with an animal.

—*Arizona Revised Statutes, §13-1411*

✦

"For certain people, after fifty, litigation takes the place of sex."

—*Gore Vidal (1925–   ), American novelist and essayist,* Evening Standard *(London, 1981)*

✦ Transcriptions ✦
of Inanity

Some of the darndest things are said both in and out of the courtroom, but the difference is that those said in court are recorded for posterity. Following are examples from actual transcripts of cases. The parties—and the lawyers—in these cases are as guilty of malapropisms as any defendant could be of charges leveled against him.

✦

LAWYER: Do you know how far pregnant you are right now?

WITNESS: I will be pregnant three months November eighth.

LAWYER: Apparently, then, the date of conception was August eighth?

WITNESS: Yes.

LAWYER: What were you and your husband doing at that time?

> —*Quoted in Mary Louis Gilman, ed.,*
> Humor in the Court *(1977)*

✦

LAWYER: Did you ever stay all night with this man in New York?

WITNESS: I refuse to answer that question.

LAWYER: Did you ever stay all night with this man in Chicago?

WITNESS: I refuse to answer that question.

LAWYER: Did you ever stay all night with this man in Miami?

WITNESS: No.

> —*Quoted in Mary Louis Gilman, ed.,*
> Humor in the Court *(1977)*

· 7 ·

Trains, Cars, and Wacky Drivers

How many times have you wanted to yell to the idiot who just cut you off: "Where'd you get your driver's license? K-mart?" Or words to that effect.

It may be hard to believe, but most drivers on the road have actually passed their state's driving test—though you'd never know that from the way they drive. Especially when they're in front of *your* car.

Think about it: Every time you get in your car to drive somewhere you are also gambling with your health and safety. You drive on a highway surrounded by other drivers, possibly in various stages of inebriation, who are piloting 2,500 pounds of steel at 70 miles per hour. (Well, it used to be 2,500 pounds of steel. With today's proliferation of four-wheel-drive sport utility vehicles, which see a lot more pavement than rough terrain, the number is more like 4,000 pounds of steel.)

Driving is serious business. Maybe you should just take the train.

Or not.

—✦ Fast Train to Nowhere ✦—

In Texas, the law states that when two trains meet at a railroad crossing, each shall come to a full stop. Is it really necessary to legislate physics?

—*Texas Civil Statutes, §6559h-11*

✦

Thank heaven for small gifts. This may be small consolation but, in Kansas, if a train runs over you, the railroad company must give your remains a free ticket on the train.

—*Kansas Statutes, §66-701*

✦

What's the last thing to go through a person's head when standing in front of a moving train? Right, his rear end. And not only that, he'd be breaking the law in Minnesota.

—*Minnesota Statutes, §609.85*

─◆"But Officer . . ."◆─

"God in His wisdom made the fly,/ And then forgot to tell us why." That pretty much sums up many people's sentiments on the worthiness of "rubberneckers" as well.

An indirect yet potentially effective approach to end the loathsome practice was taken by an Arizona court. A police officer investigating a wrecked auto noticed a driver slow to a near stop to rubberneck, and then speed away. Now, a police officer cannot pull a vehicle over unless he suspects criminal activity or the driver committed a traffic violation. But this police officer "suspected" that the driver, Richcreek, had driven, or knew about, the wrecked auto, so he chased and pulled Richcreek over. Lo and behold, Richcreek was driving a stolen vehicle.

The court held that, no, it was not an unreasonable stretch of the law to find this a reasonable stop justified by suspicion of criminal activity.

—State v. Richcreek,
211 Ariz. Adv. Rep. 25 (Arizona Ct.App. 1996)

◆

Life in the fast lane: The driver of a mortuary van, caught in the special lane reserved for car pools and buses during rush hours, was ticketed on an Orange County freeway for not having the minimum of two occupants in the vehicle.

Undaunted, the driver claimed that his "occupants" were his cargo of four frozen cadavers. His argument had a frosty reception; the judge held that the passengers must be alive to qualify.

—People v. Hanshew,
5 Cal Rptr.2d 172 (California Ct. App. 1992)
(ordered not published)

✦

A plaintiff sued a partygoer who lost control of her car and, at one-thirty in the morning, crashed into one of the plaintiff's children's bedrooms. The partygoer defended herself with the theory that the matter was covered under the Colorado No-Fault Act, which covered accidents suffered by "pedestrians." The court, unimpressed by the defendant's tortured stretch of logic, held that pedestrians are found walking public roadways, not lying in bed at home.

—Smith v. Simpson,
648 P.2d 677 (Colorado Ct. App. 1982)

◆ It's the Law ◆

You are guilty of reckless driving in the state of Washington if you cannot embrace another and still operate the vehicle freely and unhampered. Is this maneuver on the driving test?

—*Revised Code of Washington, §46.61.665*

◆

Oklahoma requires the driver of a car involved in a vehicular homicide to stop his car immediately and give his name, address, and vehicle registration "to the person struck." Apparently the Oklahoma legislature knows of a ledger of St. Peter's that the rest of us don't.

—*Oklahoma Statutes, §47-10-104*

✦

In Texas, a drink in the car is so ubiquitous that it has its own nickname, a "roadie." But the state of Washington has gone further. No front seat TVs in that state, no matter how gripping the soap opera.

—*Revised Code of Washington, §46.37.480*

✦

Even the parking meters of Mesa, Arizona, are protected: You are not allowed to shove a slug (or a phony coin) into one.

—*Mesa (Arizona) City Code, §10-2-7*

✦

A New York woman challenged the revocation of her driver's license by the commissioner of the Department of Motor Vehicles as excessive punishment. Though she was unsuccessful in her protest, the commissioner ruled that she could reapply for her license after thirty days.

Her misdeed? She intentionally ran over her husband, killing him. It seems that soon after she and her new husband had left their wedding reception, he got out of the car, splayed himself in front of it, and told her to drive over him. She obliged.

—Bonitatibus v. Melton,
74 A.D.2d 975, 426 N.Y.S.2d 188
(New York. App. Div. 1980)

8

Crimes and Criminals

Many years ago Art Linkletter wrote a book called *Kids Say the Darnedest Things.* The book sold millions of copies, because everyone wanted to laugh at some of the silly things that came out of kids' mouths.

Well, it's not just kids. And it's not just saying things, but doing them, too. The mind boggles just thinking about some of the bizarre behavior people expect to get away with.

Below, some of the strangest things people have said and done in a courtroom.

✦Thief Relief✦

A man who botched his burglary at a Charlotte, North Carolina, bank sued the bank for $15 million. Amil Dinsio, fifty-eight, had tried—and failed—to carve a hole in the roof of the United Carolina Bank in 1992. He was caught, and then he filed a $15 million lawsuit. The basis of his complaint: The bank overstated the amount it could have lost in the break-in, causing poor Dinsio to spend too much time in a federal prison.

Why $15 million? That's "just a figure," Dinsio said. "It's what you do in lawsuits."

—Dinsio v. United Carolina Bank,
Case no. 3: 94CV161-MU (W.D. North Carolina 1994)

✦

The facts of a case often require no embellishment. A minor once used her girdle to hide shoplifted merchandise in the state of New York. She was charged with using her girdle as a burglary tool. The court wrote:

> Is a girdle a burglar's tool or is that stretching the plain meaning of Penal Law Sec. 140? This elastic issue of first impression arises out of a charge that the respondent shoplifted certain items . . . by dropping them into her girdle.
>
> Basically [the prosecutor] argues that the respondent used her girdle as a kangaroo does her pouch, thus adapting it beyond its maiden form. The [public defender] snaps back charging that with this artificial explanation of Sec. 140's meaning, the foundation of . . . counsel's argument plainly sags.
>
> —Matter of Charlotte K., *102 Misc 2d. 848 (1980)*

A homeless woman was convicted of a felony after confessing to stealing merchandise priced at $299 from a Bon Marché store. But she appealed the conviction, arguing that the same merchandise cost less than the felony minimum of $250 at a nearby Nordstrom store.

The state of Washington Supreme Court agreed with her and overturned the conviction, finding that value is determined by market—not retail—price. The court seemed to be fashioning a new doctrine of "comparison shoplifting."

Dissenting Justice Richard P. Guy observed, "A thief, at a minimum, should comparison shop before, not after, he or she decides to steal."

—State v. Kleist,
126 Washington 2d 432, 895 P.2d 398 (1995)
(Guy, J. dissenting)

✦

In an opinion allowing the amendment of a criminal charge for receipt of stolen property, the judge wrote: "As Mark Twain might have put it, this is a tale about what gets into folks when they don't have enough to do."

—State v. Knowles,
739 S.W.2d 753 (Missouri App. 1987)

⸺✦Full Court Press✦⸺ in the Courtroom

How do criminal attorneys distinguish between a delusion and a hallucination? A delusion is when a criminal defendant thinks a judge will grant his motion and a hallucination is hearing the judge actually grant one: "For whatever else he may lack, [the defendant] suffers not for lack of chutzpah." That was the conclusion of an appellate judge faced with a defendant who, after being convicted for bribing a judge for $2,500, wanted to have the $2,500 refunded.

—State v. Strickland,
42 Md.App.357, 400 A.2d 451
(Maryland Ct.Spec.App. 1979)

Thumbing his nose at the police, one defendant, Robert Williams, broke into a county courthouse and stole weaponry locked up in the sheriff's office. On appeal, Judge H. Sol Clark could only describe the burglar's triumph as chutzpah. As support, he cited the definition in Leo Rosten's *Joy of Yiddish* as the gall of "one who, having killed his mother and father, throws himself upon the mercy of the court because he is an orphan." The judge reversed the conviction.

—Williams v. State,
126 Ga.App. 350, 190 S.E.2d 785
(Georgia Ct.App. 1972)

✦

Criminal defendants are typically more convinced of their innocence than convincing. Nonetheless, their criminal behavior, before or after being booked, can pin them like a bug.

The defendant in one case was on trial for murder of a prison kitchen supervisor and, when he objected to his public defender's refusal to call witnesses, went into the judge's chambers for a discussion of the matter. There, he threw a chair on his counsel's head and punched the judge.

He was later convicted and appealed on the basis that the judge and public defender could have been prejudiced against him as a consequence of his assaults. His conviction was sustained.

—People v. Hall,
114 Illinois 2d 376, 499 N.E.2d 1335 (1986)

✦

There is only one fictitious opinion (*so far*) in the National Reporter System that publishes American opinions. Despite several clues, the hoax went undetected for some time. One clue in the opinion, for example, cites a case precedent for a single word—"no." No legal reasoning, or even sophistry, just says "no." After noting that only the twin defendants knew which one was guilty of selling cocaine and the other of selling sugar as a counterfeit, the fictitious opinion continued:

> Can they hide behind their guilty knowledge? We cannot better answer that question than by quoting the eloquent language of Chief Justice Harris, speaking for the unanimous court: "No!"

—Commercial Printing Co. v. Lee,
262 Arkansas 87, 553 S.W.2d 270 (1977)

-✦Guilty Guilty Guilty?✦-

Stephen Mobley walked into a Domino's Pizza Store and, after cleaning out the cash register, shot the store manager in the back of the neck. Following numerous other armed robberies, Mobley was arrested.

His defense? His genes made him do it. His lawyers claimed that inherited chemical imbalances were the root cause of aggressive behavior not only in Stephen, but in other members of his violent family. One of his cousins recalled being told by her mother, "Be so glad that you are a Mobley, and you won't ever have to marry one." Mobley ultimately lost his then-novel claim that he was born without control over his actions.

—Mobley v. State, *265 Georgia 292, 455 S.E.2d 61 (1995)*

✦

American trial lawyer Clarence Darrow once defended a man on trial for criminal mayhem. On cross-examination of the prosecution's chief eyewitness, Darrow inquired, "You testified for the state that my client bit off the victim's ear in a fight, but you didn't actually see him bite off the ear, did you?"

The witness said, "No, I really didn't see it."

Emboldened, Darrow broke a cardinal rule of cross-examination. He proceeded to ask the question to which he didn't have the answer. "Well, then," Darrow said, "how do you know he bit off his ear?"

"Because I seen him spit it out," the witness said.

—*Clarence Darrow (1857–1938), American lawyer,*
Clarence Darrow, The Story of My Life *(1932)*

──◆ More Transcriptions ◆── of Inanity

Still more examples from actual transcripts of cases. Read 'em and weep—or laugh.

LAWYER (TO CHILD WITNESS): And lastly, Gary, all your responses must be oral. O.K.?

WITNESS: Oral.

LAWYER: How old are you?
CHILD: Oral.

—*Quoted in Richard Lederer,*
Anguished English *(1987)*

✦

LAWYER: Were you acquainted with the
decedent?
WITNESS: Yes, sir.
LAWYER: Before or after he died?

—*Quoted in Mary Louis Gilman, ed.,*
Humor in the Court *(1977)*

✦

LAWYER (QUESTIONING HIS OWN CLIENT, THE
PLAINTIFF, IN A PERSONAL INJURY SUIT):
What doctor treated you for the injuries
you sustained while at work?
PLAINTIFF: Dr. J ———.
LAWYER: And what kind of physician is
Dr. J———?
PLAINTIFF: Well, I'm not sure, but I
remember you said he was a good
plaintiff's doctor.

—*Quoted in Rodney Jones, Charles Sevilla, and
Gerald Uelman, eds.,* Disorderly Conduct *(1987)*

✦

LAWYER: Are you qualified to give a urine sample?

WITNESS: Yes, I have been since early childhood.

—*Quoted in Richard Lederer,*
Anguished English *(1987)*

✦

LAWYER: How many times have you committed suicide?

WITNESS: Four times.

—*Quoted in Mary Louis Gilman, ed.,*
Humor in the Court *(1977)*

✦

LAWYER: Doctor, how many autopsies have you performed on dead people?

WITNESS: All my autopsies have been performed on dead people.

—*Quoted in Richard Lederer,*
Anguished English *(1987)*

✦

LAWYER: I understand you're Jerry Lee's mother.

WITNESS: Yes.

LAWYER: How long have you known him?

> —*Quoted in Rodney Jones, Charles Sevilla, and Gerald Uelman, eds.,* Disorderly Conduct *(1987)*

✦

LAWYER: How did you happen to go to Dr. Cherney?

WITNESS: Well, a gal down the road had had several of her children by Dr. Cherney, and said he was really good.

> —*Quoted in Mary Louis Gilman, ed.,* Humor in the Court *(1977)*

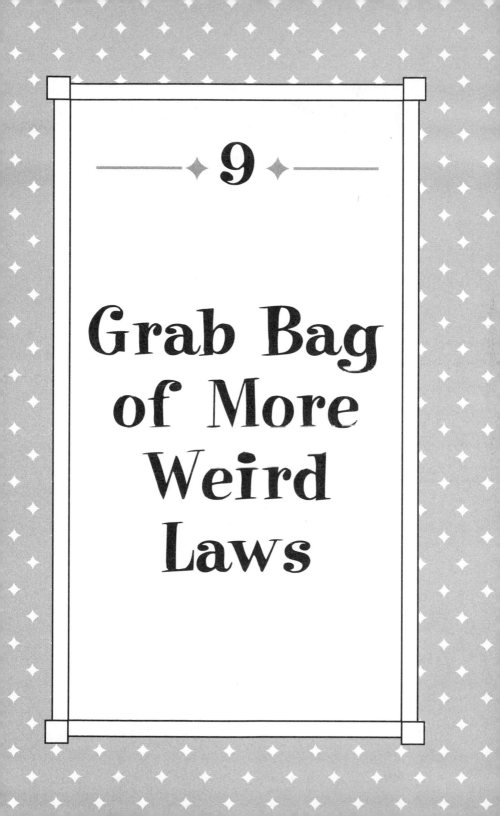

9

Grab Bag of More Weird Laws

s the journalist I. F. Stone once remarked, "It's not what's illegal that's outrageous—it's what's legal." Although he was commenting on legal loopholes, in a larger sense Stone's observation embraces much of the output of American legislative bodies. Every so often our dear legislators pass laws essentially repealing gravity or, failing that, human nature. More often than not, the rest of us wonder if they know what human nature *is*.

In this chapter you'll find actual laws that defy logic. All topics under the sun are covered and they emanate from all states of the Union.

───✦ Strange But True ✦───

No matter how tempting it may be, don't dispose of your trash in a charity donation receptacle in Washington. It's a misdemeanor there.

—Revised Code of Washington, §9.91.130

✦

Robert Frost may have received a frosty reception from Rhode Island for having penned the line, "Good fences make good neighbors." There, a fence unnecessarily higher than six feet constitutes a private nuisance if erected or maintained just to spite your neighbors.

—General Laws of Rhode Island, §34-10-20

✦

It seems the honor code will be needed to enforce this one: Funeral directors in Nevada can be arrested for using profane language in the presence of a "dead human body."

—Nevada Revised Statutes, §642.480

✦

In Maine, a person is guilty of a crime if he intentionally deposits a stink bomb on another's property. So think again if you'd like to leave two-week-old lobster under your hated neighbor's porch.

—*Maine Revised Statutes, 17-A §1003*

✦

Further restricting recreational activities, a California statute now makes it a misdemeanor in that state to look through a peephole into a bathroom with the intent to invade the privacy of the person inside. (Is there another intent?)

—*California Penal Code, §647 (k)*

✦

You can be charged with a crime in Nevada for "cheating" at a gambling game, but not in marriage.

—*Nevada Revised Statutes, §465.083*

✦

In Montana, cities are empowered to legislate good manners by making sure women can't obstruct the view of moviegoers by wearing a bonnet.

—*Montana Code, §7-5-4104*

✦

It's illegal in Virginia to throw water balloons from a multistory building. But not from trees, planes, or bridges, or just from hillsides or the street.

—*Code of Virginia, §18.2-51.3*

◆ Would You ◆ Believe . . . ?

One case certainly stands out as a benchmark for legal illogic. An Englishman bet a bystander once that he would jump from the Hammersmith Bridge. He did, and was charged with (1) causing an obstruction, (2) being drunk and disorderly, (3) attempting suicide, (4) conducting the business of a street bookmaker, and (5) endangering the lives of mariners. Convicted, he appealed to the Court of Criminal Appeal.

He needn't have bothered. In his decision, L. J. Frog wrote a classic "outcome-determinative" opinion:

It is a principle of English law that a person who appears in a police court has done something undesirable, and citizens who take it upon themselves to do unusual actions which attract the attention of the police should be careful, . . . for it is intolerable that the police should be put to the pains of inventing reasons for finding them undesirable. I have come to the conclusion that this appeal must fail. It is not for me to say what offence the appellant has committed, but I am satisfied that he has committed some offence, for which he has been most properly punished.

—Rex v. Haddock,
Misl. Cas. C. Law 31 New York (Herbert ed. 1927)

✦

Perpetual tension exists between the legislative and the judicial branches of government, one making law and the other deciding whether it should be enforced. This balancing act is best captured in this tongue-in-cheek observation by Judge James Jordan, in a case testing whether the defendant could be tried under a statute for murder of the victim, Garnett:

"From which mortal wound he, the said Hurva Garnett, then and there died, contrary to the form of the statute."

—Potter v. State,
162 Indiana 213, 70 N.E. 129 (1904)

◆

Arizona's statute for definitions states that when the law refers to a "person," this person can be seven things, including, for example, a corporation, and, oh yes, even an actual person.

—*Arizona Revised Statutes, §1-215*

——◆ Injudicious Injury ◆——

Sleepwalkers, beware! In Oklahoma, it is illegal to trespass at night and injure melons.

—*Oklahoma Statutes, Title 21 §1772*

◆

You can't molest food fish or shellfish in Washington.

—*Revised Code of Washington, §75.12.070*

✦

It's illegal in South Carolina to walk on the State House roof (but presumably okay to skip).

—*Code of Laws of South Carolina, §10-11-10*

✦

California youth will have to find new thrills, since it's no longer permissible there to trip horses for entertainment.

—*California Penal Code, §597g*

✦

It's unlawful in North Carolina to either conduct or participate in any dance marathon or walkathon lasting longer than eight hours, or, if that isn't punishment enough, to participate in more than one within forty-eight hours.

—*North Carolina General Statutes, §14-418*

✦

It's illegal in New Jersey to sleep in a room where drugs are sold.

—*New Jersey Statutes, §24:15-9*

10

Media and Pop Culture

How many times have you left a movie theater complaining that there ought to be a law against filming such trash? Or channel-surfed on a weekday afternoon and come across the plethora of tell-all talk shows that display human behavior with all its warts? Or picked up the latest mudslinging celebrity memoir? It ought to be illegal, right?

Unfortunately, as P. T. Barnum said it so well, "Nobody ever went broke underestimating the intelligence of the American public." It's perfectly legal to write, film, direct, publish, and produce anything, no matter how unredeeming in social value.

And judges aren't immune to the lure of the media. Why should they be? These days you never know what trendy references their opinions will contain. For some examples, read on.

—◆ Pop Culture Invades ◆—
the Judiciary

To get his point across, one federal
appeals judge went to the movies. His opinion
in an antitrust action brought by the federal
government against the owner of a chain of
movie theaters has about two hundred film
titles sprinkled throughout it. See how many
you can find in these two passages from the
opinion:

> It is the nature of free enter-
> prise that fierce, no-holds-barred
> competition will drive out the least
> effective participants in the market,
> providing the most efficient alloca-
> tion of productive resources. And
> so it was in the Las Vegas movie
> market in 1982. After a hard fought
> battle among several contenders,
> Syufy gained the upper hand. Two
> of his rivals, Mann Theatres and
> Pitt Theatres, saw their future as
> rocky and decided to sell out to
> Syufy.
>
> . . .

Immediately after Syufy bought out the last of his three competitors in October 1984, he was riding high, having captured 100% of the first-run film market in Las Vegas. But this utopia only proved to be a mirage. That same month, a major movie distributor, Orion, stopped doing business with Syufy, sending all of its first-run films to Roberts Company, a dark horse competitor previously relegated to the second-run market. Roberts Company took this as an invitation to step into the major league and, against all odds, began giving Syufy serious competition in the first-run market. Fighting fire with fire . . .

—United States v. Syufy Enterprises,
903 F.2d 659 (9th Cir. 1990)

Unexpected forms of pop culture surface occasionally in judicial opinions. One written in a biblical style spoofed Genesis 1:1–12 (King James version):

> In the beginning, Zim created the concept of the Golden Guides. For the earth was dark and ignorance filled the void. And Zim said, let there be enlightenment and there was enlightenment. In the Golden Guides, Zim created the heavens (STARS) (SKY OBSERVER'S GUIDE) and the earth. (MINERALS) (ROCKS AND MINERALS) (GEOLOGY). . . .
>
> —Zim v. Western Pub. Co.,
> 575 F.2d 1318 (5th Cir. 1978)

✦

One jurist felt compelled to draw on metaphors as old as the Bible in his opinion on a mill's alleged destruction of fish in the Roanoke River:

> Well, Fish is the subject of this story. From the fifth day of Creation down through the centuries, some of which lie behind us like a hideous

dream, fish have been a substantial factor in the affairs of men. . . . What is more expressive of failure than "A Water Haul"? . . . Everybody knows that "Fishy Smell" as well as the man "With the Codfish Eye." . . .

—*Hampton v. North Carolina Pulp Co.,*
49 F. Supp. 625 (E.D. North Carolina 1943), revised
139 F.2d 840 (4th Cir. 1944)

✦

Hip judges (is that an oxymoron?) refer to popular culture to give pizzazz to their opinions. For example, a Georgia opinion called upon the chorus of the 1944 song "Ac-cent-tchu-ate the Positive (Mister In-Between)," written by native son (Savannah) Johnny Mercer:

You've got to accentuate the positive, eliminate the negative; latch on to the affirmative, don't mess with Mr. In-Between. . . . Here there was no evidence to indicate any messing with Mr. In-Between.

—*United States Fire Ins. Co. v. Day,*
136 Georgia App. 359, 221 S.E.2d 467 (1975)

✦

Here is Chief Judge John R. Brown's decision on a lawsuit concerning whether federal law preempts a local ordinance that requires detergents to display their ingredients on a label:

> Clearly the decision represents a *Gamble* since we risk a *Cascade* of criticism from an increasing *Tide* of ecology-minded citizens. . . . It is as plain as *Mr. Clean* the proper *Action* is that the Dade County ordinance must be superseded, as *All* comes out in the wash.
>
> —Chemical Specialities Manufacturers Association v. Clark, *482 F.2d 325 (5th Cir. 1973) (Brown, C.J. concurring)*

◆

The scene is set: It's Hollywood's early years. One day, a certain woman answered her doorbell three times. On each occasion, a messenger—a dwarf and two costumed performers—delivered outrageous missives to her, then left. She, however, was preoccupied with preparing to give damaging court testimony the following day as a star witness against a film producer.

The next day the case came to trial in Los Angeles. The producer's attorney opened the defense by stating that the woman was mentally imbalanced. And when she was on the stand, sure enough, the woman was led to describe the story of her strange visitors and their messages. The producer, facing a convincing case against him, had hired the actors.

According to the writer F. Scott Fitzgerald's unused notes for his unfinished novel *The Last Tycoon*, "the jury shook their heads, winked at each other and acquitted" the defendant producer.

—*F. Scott Fitzgerald*, The Last Tycoon *(1941); unused notes from actual unreported case*

⬥ Sticks and Stones . . . ⬥

Strong evidence of the "dumbing down" of America is that cursing has become too banal. A defendant was held guilty of libel for merely calling someone a "turkey." The court found that this epithet connotes "ineptitude, dumbness, and ignorance." The defendant suffered twice: once for an unsatisfyingly meek insult and again for money damages.

—Ferguson v. Park Newspapers,
253 S.E.2d 231 (Georgia Ct.App. 1979)

✦

If the epithet cannot be factually proven or disproven, the defendant avoids liability. Thus, by calling a sports agent "a sleazebag who slimed up from the bayou," the coach of the Denver Gold professional basketball team escaped liability. It is impossible—at least to date—to prove whether someone is a sleazebag or not.

—Henderson v. Times Mirror Co.,
669 F. Supp. 356 (D. Colorado 1987)

✦

Can any conduct be considered outrageous in *New York City*?

In a New York case, the facts of a divorce were published over the objection of a party to the suit. A publisher ran three articles describing the charges and countercharges of abusive and cruel behavior and adultery contained in the pleadings. Because there was a state law respecting the privacy of litigants in such cases, the objecting spouse sued the publisher. But in order to establish intentional infliction of emotional distress, a plaintiff must show that the defendant's conduct is outrageous as measured by "the community standard." The complaining spouse had to get to court to learn what the rest of the country already knew—that New York "civility" has no bounds. The spouse lost.

—*Freihofer v. Hearst Corp.,*
65 New York 2d 135, 480 N.E.2d 349 (1985)

✦

Extreme and outrageous conduct was found lacking in a case in which the plaintiff was allegedly defrauded into disclosing his life story. He claimed that his story of awe-inspiring ambition to win a prize as the best disco dancer at his local dance club was later made into the film *Saturday Night Fever.*

—*Robinson v. Paramount Pictures Corp.,*
112 A.D.2d 32, 504 New York State 2d 472 (1986)

✦

Likewise, a newspaper defendant avoided liability for infliction of emotional distress when it published the name and address of the sole witness to a murder while the criminals were still at large. To prevail for such a claim in Missouri, presumably you must be killed first.

—*Hood v. Naeter Brothers Publishing Co.,*
562 S.W.2d 770 (Missouri 1978)

—✦ The Wit of Witnesses ✦—

In 1878, American artist James Whistler sued art critic John Ruskin for libel after the latter harshly attacked Whistler's modern style of painting, which was much inspired by Japanese art. In denigrating Whistler, Ruskin hurled one invective about Whistler's painting "The Falling Rocket, or a Nocturne in Black and Gold" that has become a nineteenth-century high-water mark in art criticism: "I have seen, and heard, much of Cockney impudence before now; but never expected to hear a coxcomb ask two hundred guineas for flinging a pot of paint in the public's face."

During the trial Ruskin's lawyer cross-examined Whistler about the canvas. "And do you ask this jury to believe that you are justified for labor of two days, is that for which you ask two hundred guineas?"

"No," said Whistler, icily, "I ask it for the knowledge of a lifetime."

Whistler won his case but was awarded only one farthing in damages.

—*James Abbott McNeill Whistler (1834–1903),*
American-born British artist, reported in D. C. Seitz,
Whistler Stories *(1913)*

✦

If it walks like a duck, swims like a duck, and quacks like a duck, it's a duck, right? Not necessarily.

KGB, Inc., won an injunction against a former employee who insisted on dressing up as a chicken. The problem was that the ex-employee was costumed as the radio station's mascot, and the station didn't want the public in San Diego to think that he still represented them. So KGB sued for breach of employment contract, unfair competition (!), and service mark infringement. The judge approved the injunction, meaning that the defendant could no longer impersonate a chicken.

—KGB, Inc. v. Giannoulas,
104 California App.3d 844, 164 Cal.Rptr. 571 (1980)

11

Courtship, Marriage, and Divorce

Babylon's ancient Code of Hammurabi, dating back some four thousand years, is recognized by historians as the earliest of "civilized laws." As one might expect, laws have changed somewhat over time. According to King Hammurabi's Code, for example, "If a married woman shall be caught lying with another man, both shall be bound and thrown into the river."

In modern times, their story would be a best-selling celebrity tell-all book, soon to be made into a TV movie of the week.

✦The Rules✦
of the Game

It continues to be a misdemeanor in North Carolina for a man and a woman to occupy the same bedroom in a hotel for *any* immoral purpose. Married or not.
>   —*North Carolina General Statutes, §14-186*

✦

In Arizona, first cousins cannot marry . . . unless they are over sixty-five. But they still may have children.
>   —*Arizona Revised Statutes, §25-101-B*

✦

A seventeen-year-old boy can get nailed for one year's imprisonment in South Carolina under its "heart-balm statute" if he seduces a maiden by a promise of marriage—unless she's "lewd and unchaste." Before or after the promise?
>   —*Code of Laws of South Carolina, §16-15-50*

✦

The ex-bassist of the Rolling Stones rock band, Bill Wyman, married his daughter-in-law's daughter, and his son married his mother-in-law's mother. No doubt a watchful eye is being kept on the Wymans by the legislators in Maryland. There, a man may not marry his wife's grandmother, nor may a woman marry her grandaughter's husband.

—*Code of Maryland, §2-202*

✦

In Florida, only married couples are allowed to live together "lewdly and lasciviously."

—*Florida Statutes, §798.02*

✦

In Washington, D.C., it is illegal to marry your mother-in-law. As if it weren't punishment enough to have two mothers-in-law.

—*District of Columbia Code, §30-101*

✦

In Nevada, a phony marriage is a real marriage if you close your eyes and believe real hard (no need for fairy dust, either). Putative marriages are recognized as the real thing.

—*Nevada Revised Statutes, §122.090*

✦

It is illegal in Alabama for a wife to transfer or mortgage her own land without her husband's approval, unless he's in prison, has deserted her, is crazy, or lives in another state.

—*Alabama Statutes, §30-4-12*

✦

The legislature of Alabama does allow a wife to keep her clothes as separate property from those of her husband. Most likely they wouldn't fit him anyhow.

—*Alabama Statutes, §30-4-3*

✦

In Michigan, it's a felony to seduce and debauch a single woman, but not even a misdemeanor to do the same to a single man.

—*Michigan Compiled Laws, §750.532*

✦

You need your spouse's permission to undergo sterilization (unless the spouse abandoned you) in New Mexico. Whose life is it anyhow?

—New Mexico Statutes, §24-9-1

———✦ Marriage Is the ✦——— Leading Cause of Divorce

Soldiers, foreign officers, and travelers should know this before embarking on a trip: To obtain a "quickie" divorce in Nevada, their spouses need only show that they have lived separately for a year.

—Nevada Revised Statutes, §125.010

✦

"When the horse dies, get off." That's cowboy vernacular for obtaining a divorce. In the not too distant past, courts were not as sympathetic to a spouse seeking a divorce. "Irreconcilable differences" was unknown and marriage was treated as a contractual obligation. A husband unsuccessfully sought to void his marriage by claiming that he had been ensnared:

> The parties . . . knew from the start exactly what they wanted. She wanted a husband with money—or money with a husband. He wanted a wife to adorn his house and insure that conjugal felicity of which fate . . . had repeatedly deprived him. . . . [T]he game law of the state provides no closed season against the kind of "trapping" of which appellant complains.
>
> —Main v. Main,
> *168 Iowa 353, 150 N.W. 590 (1915)*

✦

Another husband suffered the same fate just a few years later when he sued his wife for libel in a divorce proceeding. Anticipating the country western song by Conway Twitty and Loretta Lynn, "You're the Reason Our Kids Are So Ugly," the presiding judge noted that she "was without a vestige of feminine loveliness" and he "without a make of masculine attraction." The judge concluded his opinion:

> Parties too much alike ever to have been joined in marriage. Also too much alike ever to be separated by divorce. Having made their own bed they must lie down in it.
>
> —Kmicz v. Kmicz,
> *50 Pa. C.C. 588 (1920)*
> *(County Court, Luzerne County, Pennsylvania)*

"Mrs. Barber is the kind of wife who stands by her husband in all the troubles he would not have had if he had not married her." That was the opening sentence in an otherwise routine opinion. Clever phrasing, yes, but as Kipling's devil whispered, "Is it Art?"

The plaintiff in this lawsuit had contracted to buy property from the defendant, but the defendant reneged. Unfortunately for the plaintiff, the defendant's wife, Mrs. Barber, who was not a party to the lawsuit but who co-owned the property, had not signed either the contract for sale of land or the deed. So the plaintiff wanted the court to compel her husband to obtain his wife's signature under penalty of being held in contempt.

The court, not finding such behavior "contemptible," and reluctant like most courts to impose a mandatory injunction to require someone to perform an act, denied the order.

—Bondarchuk v. Barber,
135 New Jersey Eq. 334, 38 A.2d 872 (1944)

◆

In one lawsuit concerning a dog, the divorce decree between a couple failed to mention which spouse was entitled to their Boston bull terrier. The only issue on appeal was whether there was sufficient evidence for the trial court's finding that the dog had been a gift to the wife by the husband.

The appellate court first wrestled with the question of whether the dog's feelings or case precedents on legal title should influence its decision. Then, in closing, its opinion mused about whether the trial court, in a bow to King Solomon, should have offered to cut the dog in two, but concluded:

> The fact, however, that we may possibly have more confidence in the wisdom of Solomon than we do in that of the trial court hardly justifies us in disturbing its judgment.

The wife kept the dog.

—Akers v. Sellers,
54 N.E.2d 779 (Indiana App. 1944)

12

Taxes and Big Business

For most of the public, business law is as intriguing as watching paint dry. Not so for lawyers. Whether putting together a transaction or deconstructing a lawsuit, lawyers often find grappling with the network of laws of commerce comparable to assembling a complicated jigsaw puzzle. Finding a solution produces an epiphany. But the procedure to find that solution, ah, therein lies the rub.

An old lawyer saw holds that "If the facts are against you, argue the law. If the law is against you, argue the facts. If both are against you, pound the table and yell like hell." Business executives, who succeed in business by minimizing calculated risks, know better. As Boss Tweed, who ran New York City's notorious Tammany Hall political machine for many years in the early part of the century, observed, "It's better to know the judge than to know the law."

—✦Stranger Than Fiction✦—

First there was the terrible typographical error in which a legal secretary forgot only three things in a contract: a zero, a zero, and a zero. As a result, however, Prudential Insurance Company's collateral for its loan to United States Lines, a shipping company, was reduced from $92,885,000 to $92,885. The slight mistake was repeated on nearly one hundred documents, but Prudential's counsel, in-house and "out-house," never corrected the error.

Then United States Lines scuttled into bankruptcy. United States Lines's bankruptcy trustee sued Prudential to enforce the collateral agreement as expressly written, for $92,885. If the trustee's suit was successful in reducing Prudential's secured interest in the collateral by almost $93 million, the unsecured creditors of United States Lines, whom the trustee represented, would have nearly $93 million more in recoverable assets from which to satisfy their claims. To avoid jeopardizing virtually its entire security, Prudential *paid* United States Lines's trustee $11 million in settlement.

Prudential also incurred costly legal fees to fight off another lienholder who held a subordinate interest in the security and wanted to have Prudential's lien reduced to $92,885.

Next, its turn, Prudential sued. The law firm it sued, which was responsible for drafting the security agreement, was also counsel to the second lienholder. And the erring secretary at this law firm? As the law firm put it, "Her current whereabouts are unknown."

—*In re United States Lines,*
79 B.R. 542 (U.S. Bkty Ct. S.D. New York 1987)

✦

The first decision of Judge Burns concerning a Corps of Engineers contract for the construction of a dam was reversed and remanded. His decision, full of wordplay, began:

The dam case is back. When the case was here before, there was only a dam plan. Now there is half a dam. The chore assigned on remand by the Court of Appeals requires me to determine what sort of half dam is a good (i.e., safe) half dam and which is a bad (i.e., unsafe) half dam. This assignment may seem strange, since my efforts earlier to determine whether the dam plan was good were not even half as good as those of the Court of Appeals.

—*Oregon Natural Resources Council v. Marsh,*
677 F.Supp. 1072 (D. Oregon 1987)

✦

Much of adjudication concerns seemingly small issues that have far-reaching consequences. For the U.S. Supreme Court, interpreting even a comma in the Constitution establishes the law of the land. The Court frequently does a tightrope balancing act to rule whether a state law for the health, welfare, and safety of its citizens unduly burdens interstate commerce, which promotes national interests. But sometimes there's more to it than constitutional interpretation.

An Illinois statute required all trucks within its borders to be equipped with contoured mud-flaps, instead of the flat mud-guards permitted in all other states. This meant that truckers had to change mud-guards before entering Illinois.

The U.S. Supreme Court overturned the statute. But hidden in a little footnote was an interesting aspect of the case: The proponent of the overturned legislation was the Speaker of the Illinois state legislature. And why did he so fervently shepherd this legislation with its peculiar requirements? He owned a large block of stock in the only company nationwide that manufactured circular mudflaps.

> —Bibb v. Navajo Freight Lines, Inc.,
> *359 U.S. 520 (1959)*

✦ Corporate Carping ✦

The U.S. Supreme Court ordered Ralston Purina, the large food concern, to include in its corporate election proxy materials a shareholder proposal to "stop those awful Meow-Mix commercials."

> —S.E.C. v. Ralston Purina,
> *346 U.S. 119 (1982)*

✦

Insurance companies have long been nefarious for scrimping on claim payments. Consequently, they have enjoyed the dubious honor of having their own body of law develop around them—as defendants in "bad faith" claims. One case shows why: An insurance company alleged that it was not liable on the policy of someone who accidentally drowned while swimming. The policy barred recovery, the company claimed, because of a "suicide clause" in the policy for self-inflicted death. Its defense, a successful one, was that the deceased had died from his own acts.

—Grand Legion of Selected Knights v. Korneman,
10 Kansas 577, 63 P. 292 (1901)

✦

Question: Why won't authorities in Nevada grant a license to operate a whorehouse unless it's in a county of less than four hundred thousand people?

Answer: Because big gamblers, typically male, bring their wives, and prostitution would "interfere" with the big city casinos'—and therefore the state's—take of gambling profits. (Not to make those long, lonely stretches of highway less lonely.)

—*Nevada Revised Statutes, §244.345*

◆Tax Cases Are,◆ Well, So Taxing

Judges sometimes try to make the mundane matters of a tax case more interesting. Circuit Court Judge Goldberg used the Bible as inspiration to begin one opinion this way:

"To every thing there is a season, and a time to every purpose under the heaven: A time to be born, and a time to die; a time to plant, and a time to pluck up that which is planted"*; a time to purchase fertilizer, and a time to take a deduction for that which is purchased. In this appeal from a Tax Court decision, we are asked to determine when the time for taking a fertilizer deduction should be. *The Bible, Ecclesiastes, ch. 3

—Schenk v. Commissioner, *686 F.2d 315 (5th Cir. 1982)*

◆

And in one tax case, U.S. Supreme Court Justice Felix Frankfurter sagely wrote: "In law also the right answer usually depends on putting the right question."

—Estate of Rogers v. Helvering,
320 U.S. 410 (1943)

✦

Should kickbacks and bribes be tax deductible even though they reward illegal business practices? In another tax case a construction company gave money to the CEO of a construction management company. In exchange, the construction management company permitted the construction company to obtain a major subcontract without participating in the normal bidding process.

Though the payments by the construction company were clearly kickbacks, the Internal Revenue Service couldn't prove that they were illegal. Although the kickbacks violated laws, the laws had not been enforced.

Proving that two wrongs do indeed make a right, the kickbacks were thus held to be deductible as ordinary and necessary business expenses.

—*Byrne, Joseph,*
Tax Court Memoranda, Memo 1982-373 (1982)

✦

Better the devil you know than the fiancée you don't. This would explain one man's sentiments—until he went to tax court. Anticipating marriage, a man gave money to his fiancée so that she could pay off her debt. She then married another man and refused to return the funds.

The tax court held that although a loss resulting from theft is tax deductible, a loss resulting from misrepresentation is not. Applying the federal tax code's unique definition of fairness, the court as a result treated the man as an accomplice to—rather than a victim of—the fraud. The taxpayer was jilted twice: once by his fiancée and once by the tax court.

—Fuhrmann v. Commissioner,
18 Tax Court Memoranda 291 (1959)

Although tax cases typically concern mundane and arcane issues, occasionally a diamond in the rough will surface. Commuting to and from a job has long been established to be a nondeductible expense. Yet a Milton, Florida, woman successfully persuaded a federal tax court to allow her to deduct her travel costs. She proved that her "job" was to sell blood—she had a rare blood type—and that the travel was the only means for her to bring her profit-making product to market.

The court, however, disallowed her claim for a "mineral depletion allowance" for the minerals in her blood, finding that Congress intended that deduction only for mining activities.

—*M. C. Green,*
74 Tax Court 1229 (1980)

13

Prison
and
Punishment

An oft-quoted remark of the eminent jurist Oliver Wendell Holmes Jr. is that "the life of the law has not been logic: It has been experience." Well, as you'll see, the criminal courtroom has, for many, indeed been an experience that has defied logic. After all, as the English philosopher Jeremy Bentham observed, lawyers are "the only persons in whom ignorance of the law is not punished."

◆ Oops! ◆

On trial for aggravated robbery, Dennis Newton sat placidly at the counsel table until his alleged victim, testifying, identified Newton as his assailant. Newton sprang to his feet, accused the witness of lying, and said, "I should have blown your [*guess!*] head off." Catching himself, he quickly added, "If I'd been the one that was there."

Too late. "Everyone was pretty shocked," admitted his helpless court-appointed attorney. Given Newton's gaffe, she observed, he escaped with a relatively light thirty-year sentence.

—State v. Newton,
CF-85-2945 (Oklahoma Distr. Ct. 1985)

◆

On television Perry Mason obtained a crying confession from the true perpetrator while reading from an apparently condemning piece of paper which in fact was blank. In real life Melvin Belli kept a jury in suspense throughout a trial; they were guessing whether the package wrapped in butcher paper on his table contained his client's severed leg.

Modern courts now frown on such lawyers' tricks as too prejudicial to the jury. Not, however, Earnest Atkins's criminal court judge. Charged with aggravated robbery, Atkins was being cross-examined by the prosecutor about his prior crimes. Suddenly, with the jury listening raptuously to the prosecutor, the computer printout of Atkins's "rap sheet" began unraveling from the prosecutor's lectern. On and on it unraveled, for six feet.

The appellate court couldn't determine whether the incident was deliberate or accidental so it affirmed the lower court's conviction.

—Ohio v. Atkins,
Appeal No. C-840367 (Ohio Ct. App. 1985)

✦Cruel and Usual✦ Punishment

Certainly glitter and fast living don't come to mind when one's thoughts turn to Iowa. But for one man, "cruel and unusual punishment" did. A federal prison parolee sought to move to the Pacific Northwest, but a condition of his parole was that he remain in the federal district of northern Iowa for twelve years.

Horrified, the parolee tried to set aside the condition. No go. The court held that "it is not cruel and unusual punishment to require Bagley to serve his parole term in Iowa."

—Bagley v. Harvey,
718 F.2d 921 (9th Cir. 1983)

✦

A San Quentin death row inmate, a serial killer named Lawrence Bittaker, was fed up with his prison food. So he filed a complaint alleging "cruel and unusual punishment" because his sack lunch contained a broken cookie and a soggy sandwich.

—Bittaker v. Rowland,
C92-2286MHP (N.D. California 1992)

✦

California inmate Richard Burton alleged he suffered cruel and unusual punishment because he sustained a stomach ache after eating his chili.

—Burton v. Kernan,
CIVS 93-729GEB (E.D. California 1993)

✦

What to do if your prison cell is too cold? Sue! Sue!

Florida inmate Robert Attwood was hot under the collar to make sure that his cell was maintained at a comfortable 65 to 80 degrees F.

—Attwood v. Singletary,
*95-112-CA and 95-120-CA (Florida Cir. Ct.,
Civil Dep't. 1995)*

◆Civil Rights◆ and Wrongs

Rodney Alcala, a death row inmate in California's San Quentin prison, claimed that his civil rights were violated because his packages were delivered via UPS rather than the U.S. Postal Service.

—Alcala v. Vasquez,
C93-1402BAC (N.D. California 1993)

◆

Death row inmate Lee Max Barnett sought to elevate spite to civil rights protection. He had previously mailed to the parents of a witness who had testified against him a card declaring how happy he was that the witness had recently died in an accident.

Seeking to protect the grieving parents while still allowing Barnett access to the mails, the warden ordered that Barnett's mail be stamped with a notation that it was sent from prison. Barnett sued, claiming that the order was a violation of his civil rights.

—Barnett v. Vasquez,
SC-059860 (California Sup.Ct. 1994)

◆

Even paranoids have real enemies. In a lawsuit Kevin Howard, an inmate, accused the California Department of Corrections of implanting an electronic device in his brain to control his thoughts. These thoughts, he further alleged, were metabolized into statements that the prison broadcast over loudspeakers.

—Howard v. Department of Corrections,
C89-20013RPA (M.D. California 1989)

✦

Though he lost the above case, a persistent Howard filed another lawsuit because he hadn't been allowed to read *Hustler*, a girlie magazine. In this suit, he prevailed.

—Howard v. Department of Corrections,
C91-4324MRP (M.D. California 1989)

✦

Robert Attwood successfully brought attention to his accommodations when he filed for a writ of habeas corpus (literally, in Latin, you have the body) to get out of jail. His petition was written on toilet paper.

—Attwood v. Cochran,
96-4099 (Florida Dist. Ct., Civil Dep't. 1996)

✦

In a petition for a writ of mandamus (literally, in Latin, we command), used to order a public official or body or a lower court to perform a specified duty, Attwood complained of torture for not being able to shower in private and being served an old turkey leg that had gristle on it. Not at the same time.

—*Attwood v. Bowers,*
95-61-CA (Florida Cir. Ct., Civil Dep't. 1995)

✦

The inmates of the Suffolk County jail sued the warden for unequal treatment under law. They contended that their jailers had discriminated against Morris, a mouse kept by the inmates, which had been flushed down a toilet while other mice could roam the jail freely. With due gravity, Judge Hill wrote in his opinion:

> Morris . . . apparently was a trespasser and could accordingly be ejected by such force as was necessary although not by excessive force. It does not appear that the water pressure in the jail is excessively forceful. . . . [P]etitioners . . . appear to have themselves been

guilty of imprisoning Morris, without a charge, without a trial and without bail. Accordingly their petition is dismissed.

The court then quoted Robert Burns's tribute to a mouse that he had disturbed with his plow: "The best laid schemes of mice and men / gang aft agley."

—Morabito v. Cyrta,
New York Superior Court (1971)

◆

Judges are increasingly showing sympathy to the downtrodden. In 1984, a homeless man who slept on any one of six benches in a small park sued for violation of his civil rights and denial of equal protection because he was denied his right to vote. A federal court ruled that a legal address for voter registration could indeed be a park bench.

—Pitts v. Black,
608 F. Supp 696 (D.C. New York 1984)

◆

In a fatal brawl, one defendant named Butts, punch-drunk and punched while drunk, succeeded in having his murder conviction reversed. The appellate judge clarified Butts's participation in the brawl by stating: "From that point onward, the intoxicated Butts was thoroughly absorbed in absorbing punches from his two opponents."

—People v. Butts,
236 California App.2d 817 (1965)

◆ 14 ◆

Wills

here there's a will . . . Montaigne observed more than four hundred years ago that the weeping of an heir is laughter in disguise. Except for a *damnosa haereditas*, a damned or ruinous inheritance, Montaigne was right. The hand from the grave, by virtue of the law, can wield tremendous power. Here you'll see that when it comes to giving, some people truly will stop at nothing.

And remember this: Even if the meek do inherit the earth, a lawyer will have to probate the will.

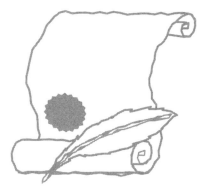

—✦ Bequests with a Catch ✦—

Heinreich Heine, considered to be one of Germany's greatest poets, was an expatriate who died in France in 1856. His wife of fifteen years, Eugénie Mirat, was by all accounts a shrew. Rather than clash with her in life, he used his will to fire a parting shot. A husband's last testament often provides for the surviving spouse on condition that she *not* remarry. Heine's will, however, closed with these words: "I leave all my estate to my wife on the express condition that she remarry. I want at least one man to sincerely grieve my death."

—Heinrelch Heine (1797–1856), German poet,
reported in Hyman, Wacky Wills
(10 Ky. St. B. J. 185 [1946])

✦

An Englishman left his widow one farthing, with directions that it be forwarded to her in an *unstamped envelope.*

—22 Case & Comment, *no. 1 p. 63 (1916)*

✦

Not to be outdone, a London man bequeathed to his wife "one pair of my trousers, as a symbol of what she wanted to wear in my lifetime, but did not."

—*36* Case & Comment, *no. 1 p. 30 (1930)*

✦

A sixpence each was once specifically bequeathed to a man and his wife so that they could each buy a halter, in case the sheriff did not have a noosed rope.

—*Hibschman,* Whims of Willmakers
(66 U.S.L. Rev. 362 [1932])

✦

Scottish novelist Robert Louis Stevenson had a young friend who once confided that she felt cheated because, being born on Christmas Day, she received presents only once a year. Drawing up his will, Stevenson remembered the girl and bequeathed his own birthday to her. Later, he modified his legacy: "If, however, she fails to use this bequest properly, all rights shall pass to the President of the United States."

—*Robert Louis Stevenson (1850–1894),*
Scottish writer, reported in Jacob Braude,
Speaker's and Toastmaster's Handbook of Anecdotes
by and about Famous Personalities *(1971)*

✦

In his will, a Canadian barrister shocked his peers by providing specific bequests of shares in horse race clubs and breweries to various clergymen. He then willed the residue of his estate in ten years following his death to "the Mother who has since my death given birth in Toronto to the greatest number of children as shown by the Registrations under the vital Statistics Act."

The Ontario Supreme Court upheld this strange bequest, noting that it was "prompted rather by sympathy for the mothers of large families . . . not unmingled with a grim sense of humour."

—Re Millar,
1 Dom. L. R. 127 (1936)

✦

The will of the jurisconsultas of Padua Lodovico Cortusio in classical Rome forbade any of his relatives or friends to weep at his funeral. Anyone found so weeping would be disinherited, and he who laughed most heartily would be the principal heir and universal legatee.

—*Julia Byrne*, Curiosities of the Search-Room *(1880)*

✦

A Mrs. Petherbridge, a Bible student and Holy Land traveler, bequeathed "the right mummy hand of Pharoah's daughter who rescued Moses from the waters of the Nile" to Bradley Polytechnic Institute.

—*28* Case & Comment, *no. 1 (1922)*

✦

A Louisville man bequeathed his widow his bathrobe because she had worn it so often when he desired it himself.

—*20* Case & Comment, *no. 1 p. 662 (1914)*

✦

One English testator with a heart of ice directed that four hundred intimate friends be invited to his funeral at eight o'clock on a winter morning. Those who attended would qualify for significant bequests.

—The Eccentricities of Testators,
15 Green Bag 583 (1903)

✦

One testator left his entire estate to the three women "to whom I owe all my earthly happiness." Oddly enough, each woman had rejected his marriage proposal.

—The Eccentricities of Testators,
15 Green Bag 583 (1903)

✦

In her will, a woman from Kentucky provided that tobacco be planted over her grave so that the leaves, nourished by her remains, could be smoked by her lamenting lovers.

—Curious Wills, *2 Green Bag 444 (1890)*

✦

Perhaps her inspiration was Omar Khayyam's historic request for grapevines to be planted on his grave.

—*Omar Khayyam,* The Rubáiyát, Quatrains
XCI, XCII *(1899)*

✦

Philip, Fifth Earl of Pembroke, bequeathed in his will "nothing to my Lord Saye, and I do make him this legacy willingly, because I know that he will faithfully distribute it unto the poor. . . . I give to Lieutenant-General Cromwell one of my words, which he must want, seeing that he hath never kept any of his own."

—*Julia Byrne,* Curiosities of the Search-Room *(1880)*

✦

The French writer Rabelais declared in his will that "I have no available property, I owe a great deal; the rest I give to the poor."

—*François Rabelais (1494?–1553),*
French writer, reported in Julia Byrne,
Curiosities of the Search-Room *(1880)*

✦

One testator directed that his creditors be his pallbearers because "they have carried me so long already." He bequeathed his bank overdraft "to my wife—she can explain it."

—*37* Case & Comment, *no. 4 (1931)*

✦

"To my wife I leave her lover, and the knowledge that I was not the fool she thought me; to my son I leave the pleasure of earning a living. For twenty years he thought the pleasure mine. He was mistaken."

—*40* Case & Comment, *no. 1 (1934)*

✦

A Canadian doctor, Dunlop, devised land to two sisters; one "to console her for marrying a man she is obliged to henpeck," and the other "because no one is likely to marry her." The doctor bequeathed a punch bowl in his will to a brother-in-law "because he will do credit to it."

—*Julia Byrne,* Curiosities of the Search-Room *(1880)*

✦

A Pennsylvania decedent bequeathed "to my son Eugene, five dollars and the world in which to make a living."

—*John Marshall Gest,* Some Jolly Testators,
8 Temp. L. Q. (1934)

✦

Another Pennsylvania testator bequeathed "to my husband, five dollars at the rate of ten cents a month."

—*John Marshall Gest*, Some Jolly Testators,
8 Temp. L. Q. (1934)

✦

Yet another Pennsylvania testator bequeathed "fifty cents to my son-in-law to buy a good stout rope with which to hang himself and thus rid mankind of one of the most infamous scoundrels."

—*John Marshall Gest*, Some Jolly Testators,
8 Temp. L. Q. (1934)

✦

A testator left a trust fund of $1,000 to be invested in order to retain lawyers to prosecute any civil matters that might arise against the testator's named son-in-law, and to assist in "prosecuting any criminal complaint that ever arose against him and, if possible, help get him hanged."

—*42* Case & Comment, *no. 1 (1936)*

✦

A German bequeathed his effects to a poor man he disliked, on condition that the legatee always wear scratchy linen underwear.

—Some Singular Wills, *15 Green Bag 430 (1903)*

✦

A Finn's will contained a devise (a gift of land) to the devil. The attempt failed, perhaps due to uncertainty as to the identity of the devisee, who failed to appear. Presumably, the testator was seeking preferment.

—*2 Green Bag 162 (1898)*

✦

A French lawyer devised Fr100,000 to a local insane asylum, declaring that it was simply an act of restitution to his clients (who had been crazy enough to engage him).

—*Virgil Harris,* Ancient Curious and Famous Wills *(1911)*

✦

A Colonel Nash left an annuity to certain bell ringers, on condition that they toll a dirge from 8 A.M. to 8 P.M. on each anniversary of his wedding day and let the bells peel on each anniversary of his date of death, which freed him from matrimony.

—Some Singular Wills, *15 Green Bag 430 (1903)*

✦

An Englishman bequeathed £1,000 to his widow, declaring that it would have been £10,000 had she let him read his evening newspaper in peace.

—Some Singular Wills, *15 Green Bag 430 (1903)*

✦

In a long rhyming will, Frenchman Paul Scarron bequeathed permission to remarry to his widow, power to alter the French language to the Academy [France's illustrious L'Academie des Inscriptions et Belles-Lettres], and 500 pounds of patience to one Corneille. Scarron's widow apparently accepted his charge; at age fifty she married King Louis XIV of France.

—The Eccentricities of Testators,
15 Green Bag 583 (1903)

✦

A scholar declared in his will "To my beloved nephew I bequeath ten thousand which he will find in a package in my safe." The nephew found a packet of 10,000 . . . chess problems, with a note promising that they would invaluably improve his mind.

—*John De Morgan*, Whimsical Wills,
21 Green Bag 152 (1909)

A French testator once left his entire
estate to a nearby Jesuit monastery on condition that upon the return of the testator's son
from abroad, the son should inherit "the sum
which the fathers shall choose." The son
returned, asked for his share, and, dissatisfied
with what the fathers gave him, sued.

His advocate argued that the provision "the
sum which the fathers shall choose" was to go
to the son; thus the son should get the part the
fathers had chosen for themselves. The court
agreed and ordered the bulk of the estate given
to the son.

—*James Croake,* Curiosities of Law
and Lawyers

✦

In William Shakespeare's will, he made
only one reference to his wife: "I give unto my
wife my second best bed, with the furniture."

—*Virgil Harris,* Ancient Curious and
Famous Wills *(1911)*

✦

A childless husband legally adopted his wife as his child to enable her to take the entire remainder interest in a Kentucky trust fund established by his mother and bequeathed "to his heirs at law."

—Bedinger v. Graybill's Executor,
302 S.W. 2d 594 (Kentucky 1957)

———◆ Wills That Don't ◆——— Stand on Ceremony

With touching irony, an insolvent testator made out his will on the back of a dunning letter from a creditor.

—*John Marshall Gest*, Some Jolly Testators,
8 Temp. L. Q. 297 (1934)

◆

It is a truism that doctors' handwritings are illegible except to a few noted archaeologists moonlighting as pharmacists. Yet, adding insult to injury, one physician made out his will on the back of a prescription blank containing his office hours.

—*John Marshall Gest*, Some Jolly Testators, *8 Temp. L. Q. 297 (1934)*

✦

Smith Gipson said, "I'd like to see them lawyers find a blowhole in that"—his two thousand-word will contained no punctuation marks. The will was probated after the judge supplied his own punctuation.

—9 Law Student, *No. 2, p. 27 (1932)*

✦

Wishful thinking: A Rochester, England, woman instructed that her coffin have a lock and key, with the key placed in her dead hand so she could release herself at her pleasure.

—*Sir George Gomme*, Folklore as an Historical Science *(1908)*

✦

Food for thought: A woman's recipe book contained a long recipe that concluded with the words, "Measure tomatoes when peeled. In case I die before my husband I leave everything to him." [signed].

—*John Marshall Gest,* Some Jolly Testators, *8 Temp. L. Q. 297 (1934)*

✦

In California, a court upheld the will of G. W. Hazeltine, an elderly hospital patient. He had written it on his nurse's petticoat.

—Pelkey v. Hodge, *112 California App. 424 (1931)*

Disposal of the Testator's Body

Jilted as a lover, a testator instructed that his body be boiled down, and the residual fat be made into a candle. It would be delivered after dark to his beloved, so that by its light she could read a note in which he had avowed his, ah, burning devotion.

—*Julia Byrne,* Curiosities of the Search-Room *(1880)*

✦

A Hussite chief who died in 1424, Johann Ziska, requested that his skin be fashioned into a drumhead so that pounding on his remains would scare away tribal enemies.

—*Julia Byrne,* Curiosities of the Search-Room *(1880)*

✦

A French man instructed that his body be burned by the Paris Gas Company. Prior to dying in 1895, the testator modestly declared, "I have used my mental power to enlighten the public, and I desire that my body be used to enlighten the people after my death."

—The Eccentricities of Testators,
15 Green Bag 583 (1903)

✦

An American testator willed his corpse to Harvard for anatomy purposes, and provided that his skin be made into drumheads on which "Yankee Doodle" was to be played at Bunker Hill each June 17.

—*John De Morgan,* Wills—Quaint, Curious and Otherwise, *13 Green Bag 567 (1901)*

✦

Philosopher Jeremy Bentham, in a most friendly gesture, bequeathed his body to a friend. After dissecting it for medical students, the friend preserved the skeleton, padded it until it could wear Bentham's clothes, and placed it in a mahogany case with a plate-glass front. Bentham's corpse, as it were, "presided" over subsequent medical discussions.

—*Jeremy Bentham (1748–1832), British philosopher, reported in Julia Byrne,* Curiosities of the Search-Room *(1880)*

✦

Some people will do anything to break into show biz. John Reed, a stagestruck gas-lighter at a Philadelphia theater, bequeathed his skull to be used in the theater as the skull of Yorick for *Hamlet* productions.

—*Julia Byrne,* Curiosities of the Search-Room *(1880)*

✦

The will of Richard I of England provided that different parts of his body be buried in three different locations.

—*106* Law Times Journal *(England) 415 (1899)*

✦

One testator devised his estate to a total stranger and directed that part of his body "be converted into fiddle strings."

—*John Proffatt,* Curiosities and Law of Wills *(1876)*

✦

A Vienna millionaire directed in his will that an electric light be installed in his vault and another in his coffin. But he failed to provide for extra bulbs.

—Extraordinary Wills, *10 Green Bag 444 (1890)*

——◆ The Disinclined ◆—— Disinherited

One father (a man who, when his son had a date scheduled with a young lady, would let the air out of the lovelorn's tires) disinherited his family. But first he announced he would do so in a newspaper advertisement.

> —In the Matter of the Estate of Raney,
> *799 P.2d 986 (Kansas 1990)*

◆

The niece of a testator challenged his will, in which he had disinherited her. Her basis was that he lacked capacity because he dressed conservatively, was forgetful on occasion, and left his socks on the floor. Though "interesting tidbits," the court disagreed with her diagnosis.

> —In Re Estate of Weir,
> *475 F.2d 988 (District of Columbia Cir. 1973)*

15

Lawyers

Many lawyers treat the law as a crusade. They comfort the afflicted and afflict the comfortable. They see a perverse logic to the law, yet are frustrated by poorly aimed or drafted legislation. The law often speaks in italics and exclamations, not reason.

Lawyers are part of the problem. Addicted to legalese, they are obtuse, redundant, and verbose. Judges, too, are afflicted, affected, and infected; for example, they "order, adjudge, and decree" rather than just grant motions.

No doubt an ability to speak the speech is important for success in, and even access to, the legal system. Just ask anyone who has been a defendant in a lawsuit. Or a plaintiff. The legal system is like a besieged city: Everybody outside wants in, and everybody inside wants out. T'were it ever thus.

—✦Stranger Than Fiction✦—

The district attorney in Missouri got carried away with his invective against the defendant he was prosecuting: "[He] ought to be shot through the mouth of a red hot cannon, through a barb wire fence into the jaws of hell," and then "he ought to be kicked in the seat of the pants by a Missouri mule and thrown into a manure pile to rot."

—State v. Richter,
36 S.W.2d 954 (Missouri Ct.App. 1931)

✦

Some attorneys are so clever in outwitting themselves that they can have a traffic ticket reduced to a charge of manslaughter. An attorney filed over forty frivolous lawsuits and appeals over his ten-year career before the court ordered him disbarred. Some examples? He sued to have certain forms used by the federal district courts declared unconstitutional on behalf of all the trees of the United States. He also filed a complaint with the Pollution Control Board against an individual alleging pollution of the mind and contamination of the air due to character assassination.

—In re Jafree,
93 Illinois 2d 450, 444 N.E.2d 143 (1985)

✦

Following a successful paternity suit, an attorney filed a countersuit on behalf of his losing client. The plaintiff, he alleged, had contracted to impregnate the defendant, and had agreed that if a normal baby was born, he was entitled to receive a "stud fee." The court suggested disciplining the attorney.

—Committee on Legal Ethics of the
West Virginia State Bar v. Douglas,
370 S.E.2d 325 (West Virginia 1988) cert. den.
110 S.Ct. 406 (1989)

✦

Lawyers excel in thinking on their feet, even when the rule of law escapes them. The fiery orator and presidential contender William Jennings Bryan was arguing a case before the Supreme Court of Nebraska. He was told from the bench that the court was clearly against him on the point he was arguing. Undeterred, Bryan replied, "If the court is against me on this point, I have three others equally conclusive."

—*William Jennings Bryan (1860–1925),*
American lawyer, orator, and presidential contender,
reported in Stanley Jackson, Laughter at Law *(1961)*

✦

And, while arguing in front of the U.S. Supreme Court, the witty lawyer Joseph Hodges Choate was informed by the Court that what he was arguing directly contradicted what was stated in his brief.

"Oh well," Choate said, "I have learned a great deal about the case since the brief was prepared."

—Joseph Hodges Choate (1832–1917),
American lawyer and diplomat, reported in
Theron Strong, Joseph H. Choate *(1917)*

✦

As the complicated trial drew to a close, British barrister Lord Birkenhead, F. E. Smith, made his summation of the salient issues and facts before the slow and pedantic judge. When the judge, however, expressed his failure to grasp some of the issues, Smith made a cogent but short account of the issues and their implications. Smith sat down.

The judge courteously thanked him, but then said, "I have read your case, Mr. Smith, and I am no wiser now than I was when I started."

"Possibly not, my lord," replied the weary Smith, "but far better informed."

—*Frederick Edwin Smith, 1st Earl of Birkenhead (1872–1930), British lawyer and politician, reported in Kenneth Edwards,* I Wish I'd Said That: An Anthology of Witty Replies *(1976)*

✦ The Unclassifieds ✦

The next two stories have passed through the ages without reliable attribution to the lawyers involved:

A distinguished member of the Boston bar was arguing before the full bench of appellate judges. The presiding judge stopped him, remarking brusquely, "That is not the law, counselor."

"I beg your honor's pardon," the attorney replied suavely. "It *was* the law before your honor spoke."

✦

Distinguished barrister Sir John Maynard, then in his twilight years, was defending at a murder trial. He challenged the presiding judge, Lord Jeffreys (1648–1689), a renowned bully who became chief justice and chancellor, on a point of law.

"Sir," the judge said, "you have grown so old you have forgotten the law."

"I have forgotten more law than you ever knew," Maynard said. "But allow me to say, I have not forgotten much."

—*Sir John Maynard (1602–1690), English lawyer*

✦

"Lawyers, I suppose, were children once."

—*Charles Lamb (1775–1834), English writer, quoted in W. H. Auden and Louis Kronenberger, The Viking Book of Aphorisms (1962)*

✦

"[I] would be loth to speak ill of any person who I do not know deserves it, but I am afraid he is an attorney."

—*Samuel Johnson (1709–1784), English lexicographer and wit, quoted in James Boswell, The Life of Samuel Johnson (1791)*

✦

Following the after-dinner speech of American playwright George Ade, a famed lawyer, with his hands buried in his pants pockets, began his speech: "Doesn't it strike the company as a little unusual that a professional humorist should be funny?"

Ade waited for the laughter to die down before replying: "Doesn't it strike everyone as a little unusual that a lawyer should have his hands in his own pockets?"

—George Ade (1866–1944), American humorist
and playwright, reported in Jacob Braude,
Speaker's and Toastmaster's Handbook of Anecdotes
by and about Famous Personalities *(1971)*

✦

"Never was an item so openly sold as the perfidy of lawyers."
—Tacitus (c. 56–c. 117), Roman senator and historian
Annals *(1959)*

✦

This house, where once a lawyer
    dwelt
Is now a smith's. Alas!
How rapidly the iron age
Succeeds the age of brass!
—*John Erskine (1695–1768), Scottish jurist and*
            professor, quoted in Marshall Brown,
    Wit and Humor of the Bench and Bar *(1899)*

✦

"The devil makes his Christmas-pies of
Lawyers' tongues and clerks' fingers."
                —*Thomas Adams (1807–1874),*
                American clergyman and poet,
    The Works of Thomas Adams (Sermons) *(1862)*

✦

Why is there always a secret sing-
    ing
When a lawyer cashes in?
Why does a hearse horse snicker
Hauling a lawyer away?
—*Carl Sandburg (1878–1967), American poet and*
        writer, "The Lawyers Know Too Much"
                in Complete Poems *(1950)*

✦

When American lawyer and politician Chauncey Depew was quite old, he was sitting at dinner next to a young woman who was wearing an off-the-shoulder dress of extreme cut. Depew, who couldn't help eyeing her décolletage, finally leaned toward her, and whispered, "My dear girl, what is keeping that dress on you?"

"Only your age, Mr. Depew."

—Chauncey Mitchell Depew (1834–1928), American lawyer and politician, reported in Isaac Asimov, Isaac Asimov's Treasury of Humor *(1971)*

✦

A reporter had the temerity to ask legendary lawyer Clarence Darrow for a prepared copy of a speech he was to give later that evening. Irritated, Darrow handed him a blank piece of paper and turned his heel.

"But Mr. Darrow," the reporter called out, "this is the same speech you gave last week."

—Clarence Darrow (1857–1938), American lawyer, reported in Robert Hendrickson, American Literary Anecdotes *(1990)*

✦

"Two lawyers can live in a town where one cannot."

—*Proverb, in Vincent Lean,* Lean's Collectanea *(1902–1904)*

✦

"The first thing we do, let's kill all the lawyers."

—*William Shakespeare (1564–1616), British playwright and poet, in* King Henry VI, Part II, Act IV, sc. ii *(1591)*

——✦ Lawyers' Cleverness ✦——

"A lawyer is a man who profits by your experience."

—*Anonymous*

✦

"A lawyer is someone who helps you get what's coming to him."
—*Anonymous (Attributed to Oscar Levant.)*

✦

"If there were no bad people there would be no good lawyers."
—*Charles Dickens (1812–1870), English writer, in*
The Old Curiosity Shop (1841)

✦

"I don't know as I want a lawyer to tell me what I cannot do. I hire him to tell me how to do what I want to do."
—*John Pierpont Morgan (1837–1913),*
American financier, quoted in Ida M. Tarbell,
The Life of Elbert H. Gary (1925)

✦

"Two farmers each claimed that he owned a certain cow. While one farmer pulled on the cow's head, and the other on its tail, the cow was milked by a lawyer."
—*Jewish parable*

✦

"Lawyer. One skilled in circumvention of the law."

—Ambrose Gwinnett Bierce (1842–1914?), American writer and poet, in The Devil's Dictionary *(1911)*

✦

"His mind was like a soup dish, wide and shallow; it could hold a small amount of nearly anything, but the slightest jarring spilled the soup into somebody's lap."

—Irving Stone (1903–1989), American journalist and writer, describing politician and lawyer William Jennings Bryan, They Also Ran *(1945)*

✦

"Lawyers use the law as shoemakers use leather; rubbing it, pressing it, and stretching it with their teeth, all to the end of making it fit for their purposes."

—Louis XII (1462–1515), French king, in Charles Edwards, *Pleasanteries about Courts and Lawyers of the State of New York *(1867)*

✦

"He who is his own lawyer has a fool for a client."

—Proverb

✦

"One whose opinion is worth nothing unless paid for."

—*English proverb*

✦

"If he only knew a little of law, he would know a little of everything."

—*Sydney Smith (1771–1845), British clergyman and writer, remarking about the lord chancellor, Lord Brougham [attributed]*

✦

"Nous savons tous ici que le droit est la plus puissante des écoles de l'imagination. Jamais poète n'a interprété la nature aussi librement qu'un juriste la réalité." (We all know here that the law is the most powerful of schools for the imagination. No poet ever interpreted nature as freely as a lawyer interprets the truth.)

—*Jean Giraudoux (1882–1944), French writer and diplomat,* La Guerre de Troie n'aura pas lieu (The Trojan War Will Not Take Place), Act 2, sc. 5 *(1935)*

✦

"Self-defense is the clearest of all laws; and for this reason—the lawyer didn't make it."
—*Douglas Jerrold (1803–1851), English playwright and humorist, quoted in Marshall Brown,* Wit and Humor of the Bench and Bar *(1899)*

✦

But what his common sense came
    short,
He eked out wi' law, man.
—*Robert Burns (1759–1796), Scottish poet In the Court of Session, Edinborough, quoted in David Shrager and Elizabeth Frost,* The Quotable Lawyer *(1986)*

✦

"A jury consists of twelve persons chosen to decide who has the better lawyer."
—*Robert Lee Frost (1874–1963), American poet, quoted in Lewis and Faye Copeland,* 10,000 Jokes, Toasts, and Stories

✦ The Law ✦

"Eight points of the law:
1. A GOOD CAUSE;
2. A GOOD PURSE;
3. AN HONEST AND SKILLFUL ATTORNEY;
4. AN UPRIGHT JUDGE;
5. GOOD EVIDENCE;
6. ABLE COUNSEL;
7. AN UPRIGHT JUDGE;
8. GOOD LUCK."

*—Attributed to Charles James Fox (1749–1806),
English politician, quoted in John Campbell,* Lives of
the Lord Chancellors and Keepers of the
Great Seal of England *(1845–1847)*

✦

"He that loves law will get his fill of it."
—Scottish proverb, quoted in James Kelly,
Complete Collection of Scottish Proverbs *(1721)*

✦

"The Common Law of England has
been laboriously built about a mythical figure—
the figure of 'The Reasonable Man.'"
*—Sir Alan Patrick Herbert (1890–1971), British writer
and politician,* Uncommon Law *(1935)*

✦

"Laws are like sausages; you should never watch them being made."

—*Honoré Gabriel Riqueti, Comte de Mirabeau (1749–1791), French revolutionary statesman (misattributed to Bismarck), quoted in James C. Humes,* Speakers' Treasury of Anecdotes About the Famous *(1978)*

✦

"Law. A machine in which you go in as a pig and come out as a sausage."

—*Ambrose Gwinnett Bierce (1842–1914?), American writer and poet,* The Devil's Dictionary *(1911)*

✦

"The law is sort of hocus-pocus science, that smiles in yer face while it picks yer pocket."

—*Charles Macklin (1697–1797), Irish actor and playwright, in* Love à la Mode, *Act II, sc. i (1759)*

✦

"Law is the crystallized prejudices of the community."

—*Anonymous, quoted in Ian L. Fleming,* Goldfinger *(1959)*

✦The Appeal✦
of an Appeal

"An appeal, Hinnissy, is where ye ask wan coort to show its contempt f'r another coort."

—*Finley Peter Dunne,* Mr. Dooley Says,
"The Big Fine" (1908)

✦

As king, Philip, Alexander the Great's father, was the court of last appeal. While drunk and drowsy he once pronounced sentence against a prisoner:

After sentencing, the prisoner said, "I appeal."

The king, stirring, said, "To whom do you appeal?"

The prisoner answered, "Appeal from Philip drunk to Philip sober."

—*Proverb (the prisoner's last appeal)*
See Valerius Maximus, His Collections of Memorable Acts and Sayings, *Book 6, and Francis Bacon,* A Collection of Apothegems, New and Old *(1661) for the story behind the proverb*

✦

"Trial courts seek the truth and appellate courts seek error."

—*Anonymous*

✦

"Appeal. In law, to put the dice into the box for another throw."

—*Ambrose Gwinnett Bierce (1842–1914?), American writer and poet,* The Devil's Dictionary *(1911)*

16

Judges

The courtroom is idealized as an arena in which the Manichean forces of good and evil are pitched in battle. This notion overlooks another characterization of the goings-on in open court: open season. Yes, on occasion everyone is firing off at one another, often without first taking careful aim. Courtrooms are not always places of decorum and logic.

That's where judges come in. It's their job to keep order in the court, no matter what they have to do to get it. But the course of justice doesn't always run smooth; following you'll find some of the ways judges' patiences have been tried over the years.

✦Judging Judges✦

Famed Irish lawyer, later judge, John Philpot Curran was appearing at a trial in which a judge of the high court, perhaps as an intentional slight, bent down conspicuously and began to pet his dog, which he occasionally brought into the courtroom.

Curran stopped speaking. The judge looked up inquiringly.

"I beg your pardon, my lord," Curran said. "I thought your lordships were in consultation."

—John Philpot Curran (1750–1817), Irish lawyer and jurist, reported in W. Davenport Adams, Treasury of Modern Anecdotes *(1886)*

✦

Of course, for some inexplicable reason, judges often get the last word. A young lawyer, awestruck in his first appearance before England's high court, could only stammer, "My lord, my unfortunate client—my lord, my unfortunate client—my lord—"

"Go on, sir, go on," said the Lord Chief Justice Edward Law Ellenborough. "As far as you have proceeded hitherto, the court is entirely with you."

—Edward Law Ellenborough, 1st Baron (1750–1818), British lawyer and jurist, reported in Leonard Russell, English Wits *(1940)*

✦

A young lawyer was addressing the U.S. Supreme Court for the first time. He sought to flatter the Chief Justice by saying that he had reached the "acme of judicial distinction."

"The acme of judicial distinction," replied Chief Justice John Marshall, "means the ability to look a lawyer straight in the eye for two hours and not hear a damned word he says."

—John Marshall (1755–1835), American jurist,
reported in Albert Jeremiah Beveridge,
Life of Marshall *(1944)*

✦

Just what constitutes an abuse of discretion by a judge? And just how difficult is it to enforce a judgment?

Prior to 1900, the city of Chicago used Lake Michigan both as a source of drinking water and a sewage disposal site. To remedy this unpotable situation, the Sanitary District of Chicago constructed a channel and other waterworks that made the Chicago River run backward. Chicago's sewage would thus flow into the Desplaines River, thence into the Illinois River, and finally into the Mississippi River.

States surrounding the Great Lakes, together with the United States and Canadian governments, sought an injunction against Chicago for restraining water into Lake Michigan as an impediment to navigation. Chicago was supported by the "River States," which appreciated the increased water flow of the Mississippi, regardless of its contents.

District Judge Kenesaw Mountain Landis of Chicago heard the bill in equity. Noting that "I like to drink clean water," Judge Landis kept the case under advisement for eight years(!). When he stepped down to become "czar" of big league baseball, there had still been no final decision. Ultimately, the U.S. Supreme Court confirmed the War Department's veto power over the project. The Chicago River, however, still flows backward.

—*Sanitary District of Chicago v. United States,*
266 U.S. 405 (1925)

✦

William O. Douglas was one of the few liberal justices left on the U.S. Supreme Court after President Nixon began packing it with conservative jurists. Douglas redoubled his efforts to protect civil liberties and the politically disenfranchised. Just before Douglas tendered his resignation following a crippling stroke in 1975, he was asked how he could decide cases when he couldn't read.

Douglas responded, "I'll listen and see how the Chief [Justice] votes and vote the other way."
—*William Orville Douglas (1898–1980),*
American jurist, reported in Robert Woodward and
Scott Armstrong, The Brethren *(1979)*

✦

U.S. Supreme Court justices have been known—rarely—to admit an error. Justice Felix Frankfurter observed that "wisdom too often never comes, and so one ought not to reject it merely because it comes late."
—Henslee v. Union Planters National Bank
& Trust Company,
335 U.S. 595 (1949)

✦

"I could carve out of a banana a judge with more backbone than that."
—*Attributed to Theodore Roosevelt (1858–1919),*
American president, after Justice
Oliver Wendell Holmes Jr.'s dissent in
Northern Secur. Co. v. United States,
193 U.S. 197 (1904)

—✦Judges' Judgments ✦— in Plain English

As unimaginable as it may seem, judges become tongue-tied, even in print. To wit, Justice Roujet Marshall:

"For some time after his death, plaintiff in error John G. Holmes worked in a brewery as an employee of Mrs. Walter, who had charge of the business for herself and children."

—Holmes v. State,
124 Wisconsin 133, 102 N.W. 321 (1905)

✦

In many opinions, judges can sound punch-drunk. But one opinion provides lawyers and nonlawyers alike a succinct course in concise writing, in this case on the law of remedies:

> Generally [punitive damages]
> cases fall into three categories: (1)
> really stupid defendants; (2) really
> mean defendants; and, (3) really
> stupid defendants who could have
> caused a great deal of harm by their
> actions but who actually caused
> minimal harm.

—TXO Production Corp. v. Alliance Resources Corp.,
419 S.E.2d 870 (West Virginia 1992)

✦

While most judges bemoan the decline in the moral fabric of our country, a judge some years back was instead concerned about the decline in quality of robbery demands:

> It is a sad commentary on contemporary culture to compare "Don't say a word, don't say a mother-******* word," with "Stand and deliver," the famous salutation of Dick Turpin and other English highwaymen. It is true that both salutations lead to robbery. However, there is a certain rich style to "Stand and deliver." . . . The speech of contemporary criminal culture has always been a rich source of color and vitality to any language.
>
> —People v. Benton,
> *142 Cal. Rptr. 545 (California Ct. App. 1978)*

✦

Commenting that jury instructions in simple English should replace those in rote legalese used by the lower court, a Georgia appeals court said, "A famous playwright once

said that judges' instructions are 'grand con-
glomerations of garbled verbiage and verbal
garbage.' "

—State Highway Dept. v. Price,
123 Georgia App. 655, 182 S.E.2d 175 (1971)

✦

Only a lawyer could write a document
of more than ten thousand words and call it a
"brief." In a securities case one party had
written in its brief: "The duty owing from
defendants to plaintiffs in the abstract will
vary, under *White*, relative to the juxtaposition
of the real world environmental encasement of
the two sides. The concept of causation would
seem less plastic." The exasperated court
admonished: "Briefs should be written in the
English language!"

—Gottreich v. San Francisco Investment Corporation,
552 F.2d 886 (9th Cir. 1977)

✦

Faced with the same problem in
another case, the judge opted for a different
lesson. Quoting the "immortal words" of the
chain-gang boss in the film *Cool Hand Luke*,
the 11th Circuit Court of Appeals reviewed the
argument that a special verdict was designed to

be a "doubt eliminator" as: "What we have here is a failure to communicate."

—Delaney's Inc. v. Illinois Union Insurance Co.,
894 F.2d 1300 (11th Cir. 1990)

——◆ Memorable Dissents ◆——

Although dissents do not carry the weight of law, they are often written pointedly with an aim to change the law in the future. In a school desegregation case, the dissenting judge wrote:

> This is a ghost story, a tale better suited for campfires and dark, stormy nights than for the pages of the Federal Reporter. . . . It is a story of the Fifth Circuit . . . acting more like a child whistling in the dark than a court of justice, afraid to look

out the window and see if the
mournful cries actually emanate
from somebody or are just the products of a frightened imagination.
—Jones v. Caddo Parrish School Board,
704 F.2d 206 (5th Cir. 1983) (Goldberg, J. dissenting)

✦

A dissenting judge in a case used a
brief footnote in arguing that the majority had
made the same mistake in two earlier cases,
with poor results: "There was an old saying in
Chickasaw County where I grew up, 'You ain't
learned nothing the second time a mule kicks
you.'"
—Gill v. State,
488 So.2d 801 (Mississippi 1986)
(Hawkins, J. dissenting)

✦

The majority of a federal appeals court
held that a public utility contract did not specifically provide for the situation before the
court. Dissenting Judge MacKinnon observed:

> This argument is reminiscent
> of the man arrested for walking on
> the courthouse lawn where the sign
> said, "Keep Off the Grass." In

defense he argued, "But the sign doesn't say positively."

—Holyoke Water Power Co. v. F.E.R.C.,
799 F.2d 755 (District of Columbia Cir. 1986)
(MacKinnon, J. dissenting)

───── ✦**The Short of It** ✦─────

If, as Polonius observed, brevity is the soul of wit, then the Supreme Court of California was witty indeed in a nineteenth century replete with long-winded opinions. A man sued for damages after falling into an unguarded hole in front of the defendant's premises. The owner of the property argued that the plaintiff's drunkenness contributed to his own injury, which would nullify the property owner's liability. The judge instructed the jury that they could properly consider this fact in determining the plaintiff's negligence. The jury found for the defendant property owner, and the plaintiff's appeal went up to the

California Supreme Court. Here is its *entire* opinion:

> The Court below erred in giv-
> ing the third, fourth, and fifth
> instructions. If the defendants were
> at fault in leaving an unguarded
> hole in the sidewalk of a public
> street, the intoxication of the plain-
> tiff cannot excuse such gross negli-
> gence. A drunken man is as much
> entitled to a safe street as a sober
> one, and much more in need of it.
> The judgment is reversed and
> the cause remanded.
>
> —Robinson v. Pioche, Bayerque & Co.,
> *5 California 460 (1855)*

✦

Even briefer was Judge John Gillis,
whose entire opinion read:

> The appellant has attempted
> to distinguish the factual situation
> in this case from that in [another].
> He didn't. We couldn't. Affirmed.
>
> —Denny v. Radar Industries,
> *28 Michigan App. 294, 184 N.W.2d 289 (1970)*

✦

Perhaps the shortest oral opinion on record has been attributed to U.S. Supreme Court Justice Harold H. Burton, at the time a judge. A defendant, convicted of murder, returned to court for sentencing. Then Justice Burton, as is customary, asked the defendant if he had anything to say before the pronouncement of his sentence.

The defendant pleaded, "As God is my judge, I didn't do it. I'm not guilty."

Replied Justice Burton, unimpressed: "He isn't, I am. You did. You are."

—*Harold H. Burton (1888–1964),*
American jurist, reported in Peter Hay,
The Book of Legal Anecdotes (1989)

——◆Three Extremes◆——

Examples of labyrinthine legal reasoning abound, but one case stands out for judicial certitude. Chief Justice Rugg of the Massachusetts Supreme Court in the early part of the twentieth century had an unusual personal style. One case concerned whether a certain Madden, runner-up to a Mr. Canty in an election, was entitled to the office because Canty had died before the election. Madden was, according to Chief Justice Rugg, who opined:

> [Canty] had ceased to exist before election day. He had vanished as a possible participant in human affairs. . . . Valid votes for election to an office cannot be cast for one who is not [*sic*] longer alive. It is equivalent to throwing away a vote knowingly to cast it for one who has passed from earth to the great beyond. . . . This is not a doubtful question. It requires no discussion of legal principles. No process of reasoning is necessary to convince the intelligence. It is axiomatic. It is not open to debate. It is obvious to everybody.
>
> —Madden v. Board of Election Commissioners,
> *251 Massachusetts 95 (1925)*

✦

Although dissenting opinions have become more discordant in recent years, majority opinions occasionally contain venom, too. A California appeals court overturned a conviction for unlawful possession of an obscene film because it found the search and seizure of evidence unconstitutional. In response to Justice Hanson's dissent arguing that the search was legal, the enraged majority filed a most injudicious opinion written by Justice Robert Thompson. Contained within was this footnote:

We feel compelled by the nature of the attack in the dissenting opinion to spell out a response:

1. **S**ome answer is required to the dissent's charge.

2. **C**ertainly we do not endorse a "victimless crime."

3. **H**ow that question is involved escapes us.

4. **M**oreover, the constitutional issue is significant.

5. **U**ltimately it must be addressed in light of precedent.

6. **C**ertainly the course of precedent is clear.

7. **K**nowing that, our result is compelled.

(See Funk & Wagnall's *The New Cassell's German Dictionary* p. 408, in conjunction with fn. 6 of dis. opn. of Douglas, J. in *Ginsberg v. New York* (1967) 390 U.S. 629 . . .)" [Boldface emphasis added.]

—People v. Arno,
90 California App.3d 505, 153 Cal.Rptr. 624 (1979)

The footnoted U.S. Supreme Court case refers the dissenting judge to a treatise on abnormal psychology in which the censors unwittingly betray their true impulses. The dictionary reference is to the word "schmuck," which is also spelled out by the first letter of each sentence in the footnote. Although the German definition of "schmuck" is "a jewel," one can reasonably infer that Justice Thompson intended its Yiddish definition—the male reproductive organ.

✦

Irish lawyer and later judge John Philpot Curran (1750–1817) was rebuked arrogantly in court by an English judge. The judge, expostulating at the legal proposition Curran was arguing before him, exclaimed, "If that is the law, Mr. Curran, I may *burn* my law books!"

Curran replied tartly, "Better *read* them, my Lord."

—*John Philpot Curran (1750–1817), Irish lawyer and jurist, reported in W. Davenport Adams,* The Treasury of Modern Anecdotes *(1886)*

◆

In a lawsuit brought on behalf of a boy who had been blinded, Judge William Willis (1835–1911) directed that the boy be lifted onto a chair so that the jury could see him properly. A young English barrister and later Conservative MP, F. E. Smith, 1st Earl of Birkenhead, represented the defendant.

"Your Honor," Smith protested, concerned about an undue appeal to the jury's sympathy, "why not pass the boy around the jury box?"

The judge rebuked Smith with a quote from Francis Bacon: "'Youth and discretion are ill-wedded companions.'"

"My lord," Smith said, "Bacon also said that a much-talking judge was like an ill-tuned cymbal."

Judge Willis frowned and said, "You are extremely offensive, young man."

"As a matter of fact, we both are," Smith said, "and the only difference between us is that I am trying to be, and you can't help it."

—*Frederick Edwin Smith, 1st Earl of Birkenhead (1872–1930), British lawyer and politician, reported in Second Earl of Birkenhead,* Frederick Edwin, Earl of Birkenhead *Vol. 1 (1933)*

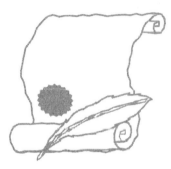

17

Poetic Justice

The phrase "the law works in mysterious ways" acquires new meaning in the examples below. Judges, lawyers, witnesses, and jurors all contribute gaffes, repartees, outrageous antics, and general roguishness to the courtroom.

Why they felt the needs to voice their opinions in verse is anyone's guess. Perhaps the cause is years of reading briefs written in "legalese." We'll never know, but we can read the results and smile.

✦

In one case in Kansas, a trial judge named Richard J. Rome wrote as a poem, to accompany an order of probation, a "Memorandum Decision" that ended with these lines:

> From her ancient profession she'd
>   been busted,
> And to society's rules she must be
>   adjusted.
> If from all this a moral doth unfurl,
> It is that Pimps do not protect the
>   working girl!

Unfortunately for the judge, the defendant he was describing as a whore was a minor; in a separate case of poetic justice, the judge was formally reprimanded for ridiculing her.

—In re Rome,
218 Kansas 198, 542 P.2d 676 (1975)

✦

Judge Burns included a poem of Lewis Carroll among others in dismissing a prosecution of a man and his son for catching butterflies in a national park:

He said, "I look for butterflies
That sleep among the wheat:
I make them into mutton-pies,
And sell them in the street."

—United States v. Sproed,
628 F. Supp. 1234 (D. Oregon 1986)

✦

David Irving was temporarily nude when he removed his wet clothes and put them in his car at Lava Beds National Monument. Charged with offensive conduct, a federal magistrate found him guilty under the statute. But a record of the proceeding, though required, was not kept. Judge McBride quoted from Irving's counsel's brief a limerick in setting aside the conviction:

There was a defendant named Rex
With a minuscule organ of sex.
When jailed for exposure
He said with composure
De minimis non curat lex.*

> —United States v. Irving,
> *No. 76-151 (E.D. California 1977, unreported)*

*[The Latin phrase is a legal maxim meaning "The law is unconcerned with trifling matters."]

✦

A plaintiff once sued for damages to a tree on his property struck by the defendant's vehicle. The entire opinion written by Judge Gillis was written as a parody of Joyce Kilmer's "Trees." Both the statement of the case and the headnotes were in verse. Yet neither the facts of the case nor the controlling law is contained in the poem. They were relegated to a footnote, one that was twice as long as the opinion itself in a case of the tail wagging the doggerel:

> We thought that we would never
> see
> A suit to compensate a tree.
> A suit whose claim in tort is
> pressed
> Upon a mangled tree's behest;

A tree whose battered trunk was
    pressed
Against a Chevy's crumpled crest;
A tree that faces each new day
With bark and limb in disarray;
A tree that may forever bear
A lasting need for tender care.
Flora lovers though we three,
We must uphold the court's
    decree.
Affirmed.

—Fisher v. Lowe,
122 Michigan App. 418, 333 N.W.2d 67 (1983)

✦

In a rare example of good poetry and
camaraderie, counsel, the judge, and even the
National Reporter System (NRS), which publishes cases, joined in the fun. The case concerned the otherwise dull issue of the court's
jurisdiction over a matter in which a sailor
sued a defendant from another jurisdiction for
his wages.

In the opinion, Judge Becker wrote:

The motion now before us
has stirred up a terrible fuss,
And what is consistently worse,
it has spawned some preposterous
    doggerel verse.

One of NRS's headnotes read:

> A seaman with help of legal sages,
> Sued a shipowner for his wages.
>
> . . .
>
> Long arm service is a procedural
> tool
> Founded upon a "doing business"
> rule.

And the defense's brief:

> For Smith, not known for his mirth
> With his knife out for
> Mackensworth
> With Writs, papers or Motions to
> Quash
> Knows that dear Harry's position
> don't wash.
>
> —Mackensworth v. American Trading
> Transportation Co.,
> *367 F.Supp. 373 (E.D. Pennsylvania 1973)*

✦

Judge Irwin wrote an ode to the country music singer Conway Twitty. Twitty chucked his Twitty Burger restaurant business but didn't chicken out on making payments to reimburse his investors. The Tax Court held that such recompense was tax-deductible, noting:

Twitty Burger went belly up
But Conway remained true.
He repaid his investors, one and all,
It was the moral thing to do.
> —Jenkins v. Commissioner,
> *47 Tax Court Memoranda (CCH) 238 (1983)*

✦

Monica Swiney had the gall to put her will in rhyme:

Of this I never will repent
'Tis my last Will and testament,
If much or little—nay, my all—
I give my brother, Matthew Gall.
> —*William Tegg,* Wills of Their Own *(1876)*

✦

Likewise John Hedges, who was truly his brother's keeper:

And I give and devise,
Much as in me lies,
To the son of my mother,
To own dear brother,
To have and to hold
All my silver and gold,
As th'affectionate pledges
Of his brother.
> —*William Tegg,* Wills of Their Own *(1876)*

✦

The Chapel Master to Elizabeth I of England, William Hunnis, had little to leave in his will except for rhyme:

> To God my soule I do bequeathe,
>   because it is his owen,
> My body to be layd in grave, where
>   to my friends best knowen;
> Executors I will none make,
>   thereby great stryfe may grow.
> Because the goods that I shall
>   leave wyll not pay all I owe.
>
> —*Virgil Harris,* Ancient Curious
> and Famous Wills *(1911)*

✦

Most long court opinions have headings to divide them into sections for better organization and comprehension. These headings offer an alternative structure for humor. One opinion, which also began with a poem, contained the headings below, tied together for your reading pleasure:

> The Procedural Background Is
>   Easily Stated,
> But the Facts Are Far More
>   Complicated—

Applying the Law Is Even Worse
But For the Reasons Stated We
   Must Reverse.

> —United States v. Ven-Fuel, Inc.,
> *602 F.2d 747 (5th Cir. 1979)*

✦

Only one field of law could be drier than tax law, and that is bankruptcy law; bankruptcy cases have to be fed drama intravenously. In one bankruptcy opinion, a judge soared on a flight of fancy based on Edgar Allen Poe's "The Raven":

> Once upon a midnight dreary,
>   while I pondered weak and
>   weary
> Over many quaint a curious files of
>   chapter seven lore
> While I nodded nearly napping,
>   suddenly there came a tapping
> As of some one gently rapping,
>   rapping at my chamber door,
> "Tis some debtor," I muttered,
>   "tapping at my chamber door—
> Only this and nothing more."

> —In re Robin E. Love,
> *61 Bankr. 558 (Bankr. S.D. Florida 1986)*

✦

V erse in opinions may refer to those who break out into song:

> Dogs will howl and cats will yowl
> When placed in congregation.
> These grating sounds may oft result
> In human aggravation.
>
> —*Columbus v. Becher,*
> *173 Ohio St. 197, 180 N.E.2d 836 (1962)*

✦

T o define drunkenness, one judge quoted Peacock's "Not Drunk is He . . . Who From the Floor" from *The Misfortunes of Elphin* to begin his opinion:

> Not drunk is he who from the floor
> Can rise alone and still drink more;
> But drunk is he, who prostrate lies,
> Without the power to drink or rise.
>
> —Pfeffer v. Department of Pub. Safety,
> *136 Georgia App. 448, 221 S.E.2d 658 (1975)*

✦

I n a case that concerned union-organiz-ing elections, a controlling precedent was named *Robbins Tire & Rubber Co. v. N.L.R.B.,* so the judge referred to it in rhyme:

> Our decision in Robbins Tire,
> Interpreting Congress's reported
>   desires,

Exposed workers to their bosses' ire.
The High Court, avoiding this sticky
    quagmire,
And fearing employers would
    threaten to fire,
Sent our holding to the funeral pyre.
—Anderson Greenwood & Co. v. N.L.R.B.,
    604 F.2d 322 (5th Cir. 1977)

✦

A Judge Scott dissented in the early
part of this century by using a fable in the form
of poetry:

One day through the primeval
    wood
a calf walked home, as good calves
    should;
But left a trail all bent askew,
crooked trail, as all calves do.
        . . .
But how the wise old wood-gos
    laugh,
who saw the first primeval calf!
Ah! many things this tale might
    teach;—
But I am not ordained to preach.
—Van Kleeck v. Ramer,
    62 Colorado 44, 156 P. 1108 (1916)

✦

Occasionally, poetry intrudes into prose, when judges embellish the facts and embowel the English language. One opinion concerned whether a taxi driver's actions while at gunpoint constituted negligence, or whether a reasonable person would instead behave coolly in such an emergency situation. The judge's flowery prose appeared in an opinion:

> There are those who stem the turbulent current for bubble fame, or who bridge the yawning chasm with a leap for the leap's sake, or who "outstare the sternest eyes that look, outbrave the heart most daring on the earth, pluck the young sucking cubs from the she-bear, yea, mock the lion when he roars for prey" to win a fair lady, and these are the admiration of the generality of men; but they are made of sterner stuff than the ordinary man upon whom the law places no duty of emulation.

The taxi driver was held not negligent. Obvious, no?

—Cordas v. Peerless Transp. Co.,
27 New York S.2d 198 (1941)

18

Just Plain Silly

For most of us, dealing with lawyers, courts, and judges isn't fun. Most lawsuits, divorces, and wills aren't sources of great merriment and elation. And how many of us jump for joy when called for jury duty? Even those people whose livelihoods are earned within the legal system often find it difficult to laugh at themselves and their profession.

So it's remarkable how much silly humor can be found in the annals of the courts. Herewith, some of the best.

◆ Twilight Zone ◆

After granting the plaintiff leave to proceed *in forma pauperis* (in the form of a pauper, i.e., a destitute person) and represent herself, Federal District Judge Fullam sized up her case as follows:

> Plaintiff names as defendants President and Mrs. Reagan, the United States Government, Congress, and the citizens of the United States and foreign countries. . . . It seems that plaintiff's basic claims are that she is god of the Universe and that citizens of the

Universe, former Presidents Nixon, Ford, and Carter, and President Reagan have perpetrated crimes against her through the use of an electronic eavesdropping device. . . . [S]he asks that the court award her items ranging from a size sixteen mink coat and diamond jewelry to a three bedroom home in the suburbs and a catered party at the Spectrum in Philadelphia.

The plaintiff didn't win.

—God, Plaintiff v. President Ronald Reagan,
1986 WL 3948 (E.D. Pennsylvania)

✦

In an unusual case, the wrong plaintiff had the right defendant. Oreste Lodi sued himself. Though most people seek to *avoid* the legal system, Lodi fashioned a novel claim to gain access to the court.

He contended that his birth certificate was in fact a certificate of power of appointment and conveyance of a trust. And since the birth certificate constituted notice of the trust's existence, he argued, he thereby became the "Reversioner" of this charitable trust. And as holder of the reversionary interest, the complaint went on, the trust would be terminated and Lodi would be vested with its assets.

When the defendant failed to answer the complaint, the surprised though gleeful plaintiff sought to enter a default judgment.

The court dismissed the complaint, noting that the pleading was a "slam-dunk frivolous complaint" and the appellate court affirmed.

—Lodi v. Lodi,
173 California App.3d 626, 219 Cal.Rptr. 116 (1985)

✦

Then there was the plaintiff who alleged that the defendant Satan (yes, *the* Satan) "on numerous occasions has caused plaintiff misery, . . . that Satan had placed deliberate obstacles in plaintiff's path and has caused plaintiff's downfall."

"We must stand completely in awe of your total lack of ignorance," noted the court, finding the plaintiff's disingenuousness in the civil rights action a little too transparent. The federal district judge, however, observed tongue-in-cheek: "We question whether plaintiff may obtain personal jurisdiction over the defendant in this judicial district."

—United States ex. rel. Mayo v. Satan and His Staff,
54 F.R.D. 282 (W.D. Pennsylvania 1971)

✦

In the eighteenth century, Baron Robert Clive was instrumental in establishing the East India Company's stronghold in Bengal. Appointed governor of Bengal, he made important reforms but was also later impeached by Parliament for widespread corruption. During the 1773 parliamentary proceedings, Baron Clive was cross-examined with a laundry list of transgressions occasioned by his subordinates and him.

Posturing defensively for mercy and no doubt lamenting missed opportunities for graft, Clive exclaimed, "My God, Mr. Chairman, at this moment I stand astonished at my own moderation!"

—*Robert Clive, Baron Clive of Plassey (1725–1774),*
English soldier and statesman,
reported in George Robert Glieg,
The Life of Robert, First Lord Clive *(1848)*

✦ Wordplay with ✦ Case Names

In the case *Short v. Long* the court resisted any pun until the end of the opinion: "The judgment of the trial court is affirmed, and that is the 'long' and the 'short' of it."

—Short v. Long,
197 Virginia 104, 87 S.E.2d 776 (1955)

✦

The court in *Plough v. Fields* dispensed with any humor in the first sentence of its opinion: "In spite of its title, this case does not involve the age old struggle of mankind to wrest a living from the soil."

—Plough v. Fields,
422 F.2d 824 (9th Cir. 1970)

✦

"Shoo Fly" is a "Mother Goose" nursery rhyme. Shoofly pie is the curious name of molasses Amish pie so sweet that one has to "shoo away" attracted flies. But shoo fly powder to shoo away drunks?

—United States v. 11 Dozen Packages of
Article Labeled in part Mrs. Moffat's Shoo Fly
Powders for Drunkedness,
40 F. Supp. 208 (W.D. New York 1941)

Repeat quickly three times: when the Faughts fought, they got what they fought for in court. A dissolution.

—Faught v. Faught,
30 California App. 3d 875 (1973)

✦

Is the courtroom virtual reality's stage for human suffering? See *Pain v. Municipal Court*, 237 California App. 2d 151 (1968); then *Anger v. Municipal Court*, 237 California App. 2d 69 (1965); and *Huerta v. Superior Court*, 18 California App. 3d 482 (1971).

✦

If that's not good enough, try *Goodenough v. Superior Court*, 18 California App. 3d 692 (1971).

——✦If the Suit Fits . . .✦——

Doctor Samuel Johnson once compared a plaintiff and a defendant to two men ducking their heads in a bucket and daring each other to remain longest underwater.

—Samuel Johnson (1709–1784), English lexicographer
and wit, reported in W. Davenport Adams,
The Treasury of Modern Anecdotes *(1886)*

✦

But the Judge said he never had
    summed up before;
So the Snark undertook it instead,
And summed it so well that it
    came to far more
Than the Witnesses had ever said.

—Lewis Carroll (Charles Lutwidge Dodgson)
(1832–1898), English writer and mathematician,
The Hunting of the Snark: The Barrister's Dream *(1875)*

✦

"Bluster, sputter, question, cavil; but be sure your argument is intricate enough to confound the court."

—William Wycherley (1640–1716), British playwright,
The Plain Dealer *(1677)*

✦

The lawyer's brief is like the sur-
geon's knife,
Dissecting the whole inside of a
question
And with it all the process of
digestion.
—*George Gordon, Lord Byron (1788–1824),
English poet,* Don Juan *(1822) canto x*

◆

"My Lord," said the foreman of an
Irish jury upon giving his verdict, "we find the
man who stole the mare not guilty."
—*T. B. and T. C.,* The New Pun Book *(c. 1906)*

◆

American financier Russell Sage, whose
fortune established the Russell Sage Founda-
tion, laid out his case before his lawyer. When
he had finished, the attorney was enthusiastic.
"It's an ironclad case," he said. "We can't possibly lose!"

"We'd better not sue then," Sage said. "I
gave you the other side's case."
—*Russell Sage (1816–1906), American financier,
reported in Jacob Braude,* Speaker's and Toastmaster's
Handbook of Anecdotes by and about
Famous Personalities *(1971)*

◆

"I was never ruined but twice: once when I lost a lawsuit, and once when I won one."

—Attributed to Voltaire (François Marie Arouet)
(1694–1778), French philosopher, writer, and wit.
Reported in Evan Esar, The Dictionary of Humorous
Quotations *(1949)*

19

Mixed Bag

Justice" and "law" are, unfortunately, not synonymous. In a continuous effort to marry the two, legislators and judges engage in an exclusive recreation, that of re-creating law.

A wretched excess of laws have been promulgated to correct past perceived injustices, in a continuing quest for justice. In this quest, legislators have often sought to regulate the absurd. But they are not the only ones who introduce absurdities into the legal realm. We've all heard about ridiculous lawsuits such as the one in which a convict who was serving extra time for breaking out of the Armstrong County, Pennsylvania, jail sued the sheriff for $1 million—for negligence in permitting him to escape. Then, there's the man rescued from a lifeboat who sued his rescuer for the loss of his glasses. The list goes on.

Here you'll find a random assortment of such absurdities.

──✦ Kids Will Be Kids ✦──

A child can't be just a child in Vermont—no whistles are allowed on children's bikes.

—Vermont Statutes, §23-1141

✦

Pity the stunted childhoods of kids growing up in Larkspur, California, where it is unlawful—unless designated or customarily used for such purpose—to climb a tree.

—Larkspur (California) Municipal Code, §9.32.060

✦

In the state of Washington, you can sell your infant to the other parent and not be guilty of a felony.

—Revised Code of Washington, §9A.64.030

✦

Also in Washington, it is the law that a babysitter can be imprisoned if he or she substitutes another child for the one the parent left with the sitter.

—Revised Code of Washington, §9.45.020

──✦School for Scandal✦──

The answer was $6.22054463335 \times 10^{-26}$. After two students learned that this answer to a homework problem (the cost of an aluminum atom on Fridays) amounted to less than a trillionth of a penny, they didn't just drop the course. Outraged by the difficulty of the mathematics in the computer programming course, the couple sought another answer '90s-style.

They sued Pace University.

And won.

The judge found "educational malpractice" on the part of their instructor, who had "unreasonably" included mathematics in the introductory programming class. The students had suffered mental injuries.

—André v. Pace University,
161 Misc.2d 613, 618 New York S.2d 975 (N.Y. 1994)

✦

Beware of sweat-drenched schools. In Montana students are exempt from appropriate exercises only on holidays.

—*Montana Code, §20-1-306*

✦

In the late 1970s a former Michigan University student sued the university and five of its faculty members for $550,000. His claim was for mental anguish that he suffered because he received a B in a German course. He felt that he deserved an A.

—*Reported in* Student Lawyer *(1980)*

——◆ Words of Wisdom ◆——

The eminent physicist Henry Augustus Rowland, known for his shy, sweet disposition and modesty, was once called to testify at a trial. During cross-examination the lawyer asked sharply, "What are your qualifications as an expert witness in this case?"

Rowland quietly replied, "I am the greatest living expert on [the matter being examined]."

Startled, the lawyer shrank, and never recovered his fumbled composure.

A friend later remarked how amazed he was at Rowland's answer—it was so out of character for such a modest man.

Rowland shrugged. "What did you expect me to do? I was under oath."

—*Attributed to Henry Augustus Rowland (1848–1901), American physicist and professor, reported in Isaac Asimov,* Isaac Asimov's Treasury of Humor *(1971)*

◆

The British wit Oscar Wilde had a homosexual affair with Lord Alfred Douglas that culminated in a sensational court case. Under questioning by the cross-examining barrister, Wilde made an irrelevant remark concerning his physician.

"Never mind your physician," interrupted the barrister angrily.

"I never do," Wilde said.

—*Oscar Fingal O'Flahertie Wills Wilde (1854–1900), British playwright, writer, and wit, reported in R. H. Sherard,* The Life of Oscar Wilde *(1906)*

◆

The Hansel-and-Gretelesque town of Carmel, California, goes to extraordinary lengths to maintain its quaintness. Women—and for that matter, men—must obtain a permit to walk the streets and sidewalks in high heels.

—City of Carmel By-the-Sea, California
Municipal Code, §8.44.020

—✦ He Should Have Been ✦— a Lawyer

The American wit Wilson Mizner made an intemperate remark during a heated argument with a magistrate. Angered, the magistrate asked him if he were attempting to show contempt of court.

Mizner responded: "No, your honor, I've been trying to conceal it."

—Wilson Mizner (1876–1933), American businessman
and wit. (Misattributed to various lawyers.)
Reported in Alva Johnston, "Legend of a Sport,"
The New Yorker (1946)

Sources

Adams, Thomas. *The Works of Thomas Adams (Sermons).* Edinburgh: J. Nichol, 1861–1862.

Adams, W. Davenport. *The Treasury of Modern Anecdotes.* Edinburgh: The Edinburgh Publishing Company, 1886.

Andrews, Robert, ed. *Concise Columbia Dictionary of Quotations.* New York: Avon, 1987.

Asimov, Isaac. *Isaac Asimov's Treasury of Humor.* Boston: Houghton Mifflin, 1971.

Auden, Wystan Hugh, and Kronenberger, Louis. *The Viking Book of Aphorisms.* New York: Viking Press, 1962.

B., T., and C., T. *The New Pun Book.* New York: Outing, 1906.

Bacon, Lord Francis. *A Collection of Apothegems, New and Old.* London: Rawley's Collection, 1661.

———. *The Essays or Counsels, Civill and Morall of Francis Lord Verulam, Viscount St. Alban.* London: John Haviland, 1625.

Barrows, Chester Leonard. *William M. Evarts: Lawyer, Diplomat, Statesman.* Chapel Hill, North Carolina: The University of North Carolina Press, 1941.

Beveridge, Albert Jeremiah. *Life of Marshall.* Boston and New York: Houghton Mifflin, 1944.

Bierce, Ambrose. *The Devil's Dictionary.* New York: A. and C. Boni, 1911.

Birkenhead, Frederick Winston Furneaux Smith, 2d Earl of. *Frederick Edwin, Earl of Birkenhead.* London: T. Butterworth, 1933.

Boswell, James. *The Life of Samuel Johnson.* London: H. Baldwin, 1791.

Braude, Jacob Morton. *Speaker's and Toastmaster's Handbook of Anecdotes by and about Famous Personalities.* Englewood Cliffs, New Jersey: Prentice-Hall, 1971.

Brown, Marshall. *Wit and Humor of the Bench and Bar.* Philadelphia: George T. Bisel, 1899.

Buckley, Tom. *Violent Neighbors.* New York: Times Books, 1984.

Bunting, Daniel George. *A Book of Anecdotes: Illustrating Varieties of Experience in the Lives of the Illustrious and the Obscure.* London: Hulton Press, 1957.

Butler, Samuel. *The Note-Books of Samuel Butler.* London: A. C. Fifield, 1912.

Byrne, Julia Clara Busk. *Curiosities of the Search-Room.* London: Chapman and Hall, 1880.

Byron, Lord George Noel Gordon. *Don Juan, canto x.* London: W. Benbow, 1822.

Campbell, John, 1st Baron. *Lives of the Lord Chancellors and Keepers of the Great Seal of England.* London: J. Murray, 1845–1847.

Carroll, Lewis (Charles Lutwidge Dodgson). *The Hunting of the Snark: The Barrister's Dream.* London: Macmillan, 1875.

———. *Alice's Adventures in Wonderland.* London: Macmillan, 1911.

Cerf, Bennett Alfred. *Shake Well Before Using.* New York: Simon and Schuster, 1948.

Cockburn, Lord Henry. *Memorials of His Time.* Edinburgh: A. and C. Black, 1856.

Copeland, Lewis and Faye. *10,000 Jokes, Toasts, and Stories.* Garden City, New York: Doubleday, 1965.

Croake, James [James Paterson]. *Curiosities of Law and Lawyers.* London: S. Low, Marston and Company, Ltd., 1896.

Currie, James, ed. *The Works of Robert Burns (In the Court of Session, Edinburgh).* London: J. M'Creary, 1800.

Darrow, Clarence. *The Story of My Life.* New York: Charles Scribner's Sons, 1932.

Davidson, Lance S. *The Ultimate Reference Book: The Wit's Thesaurus.* New York: Avon Books, 1994.

Dickens, Charles. *Oliver Twist.* London: R. Bentley, 1837–1839.

————. *The Old Curiosity Shop.* London: Chapman and Hall, 1841.

Dunne, Finley Peter. *Mr. Dooley's Opinions.* New York: Harper and Bros., 1901.

————. *Mr. Dooley Says (The Big Fine).* New York: Charles Scribner's Sons, 1910.

Edwards, Charles. *Pleasanteries about Courts and Lawyers of the State of New York.* New York: Richardson, 1867.

Edwards, Kenneth. *I Wish I'd Said That: An Anthology of Witty Replies.* London: Abelard Schuman, 1976.

Esar, Evan. *The Dictionary of Humorous Quotations.* Garden City, New York: Doubleday, 1949.

Evans, Bergen. *Dictionary of Quotations.* New York: Delacourte Press, 1968.

Evening Standard. London: May 5, 1981.

Fadiman, Clifton. *Enter, Conversing.* Cleveland: World Publishing, 1962.

————, ed. *The Little, Brown Book of Anecdotes.* Boston: Little, Brown, 1985.

Fielding, Henry. *Amelia.* London: A. Millar, 1752.

Fitzgerald, F. Scott. *The Last Tycoon.* New York: Charles Scribner's Sons, 1941. (Unused notes.)

Fleming, Ian L. *Goldfinger.* London: J. Cape, 1959.

France, Anatole. *Le Lys Rouge (The Red Lily).* Paris: Calman-Lévy, 1894.

Fuller, Edmund. *2500 Anecdotes for All Occasions.* New York: Crown, 1943.

Gilbert, Michael. *The Secret of the Missing Will.* London: Hodder & Stroughton, 1954.

Gilbert, Sir William Schwenck. *Iolanthe.* London: Chappell, 1882.

Gilman, Mary Louis, ed. *Humor in the Court.* Vienna, Virginia: National Shorthand Reporters Association, 1977.

Giraudoux, Jean. *La Guerre de Troie n'Aura Pas Lieu (The Trojan War Will Not Take Place).* Paris: B. Grasset, 1935.

Gleig, George Robert. *The Life of Robert, First Lord Clive.* London: J. Murray, 1848.

Godley, A. D., trans. *Herodotus [Histories].* London: W. Heinemann, 1921–1924.

Gomme, Sir George Laurence. *Folklore as an Historical Science.* London: Methuen, 1908.

Hansard. London: (n.p.) February 26, 1835.

Harris, Virgil M. *Ancient Curious and Famous Wills.* Boston: Little, Brown, 1911.

Hay, Peter. *The Book of Legal Anecdotes.* New York: Facts on File, 1989.

Hendrickson, Robert. *American Literary Anecdotes.* New York: Facts on File, 1990.

Herbert, Sir Alan Patrick. *Uncommon Law.* London: Methuen, 1935.

Hibschman, Henry Jacob. "Whimsies of Will-Makers," *United States Law Review,* vol. 66, p. 365.

Holmes, Oliver Wendell, Jr. *The Common Law.* Boston: Little, Brown, 1881.

Humes, James C. *Speakers' Treasury of Anecdotes About the Famous.* New York: Harper & Row, 1978.

Hyman, Herbert Hiram. "Wacky Wills," *Kentucky State Bar Journal,* vol. 10, p. 185.

Jackson, Stanley (pseud.). *Laughter at Law.* London: A. Barker, 1961.

Johnston, Alva. "Legend of a Sport," *The New Yorker.* 1946.

Jones, Rodney R., Sevilla, Charles M., and Uelman, Gerald F., eds. *Disorderly Conduct.* New York: Norton, 1987.

Keen, Judy. *USA Today.* August 5, 1994, Sec. A p. 4.

Kelly, James. *Complete Collection of Scottish Proverbs.* London: W. and J. Innys and J. Osborn, 1721.

Khayyam, Omar. *The Rubáiyát, Quatrains XCI, XCII.* Portland, Maine: Thomas B. Mosher, 1899.

234

Kipling, Sir Rudyard. *Second Jungle Book*. New York: The Century Company, 1895.

Lanman, Charles. *The Private Life of Daniel Webster*. New York: Harper & Bros., 1852.

Lean, Vincent Stuckey. *Lean's Collectanea*. Bristol, England: J.W. Arrowsmith, 1902–1904.

Lederer, Richard. *Anguished English*. New York: Laurel, 1987.

Leslie, Anita. *The Remarkable Mr. Jerome*. New York: Holt, 1954.

Lincoln, Anthony L. J., and McEwan, Robert Lindley, eds. *Lord Eldon's Anecdote Book*. London: Stevens & Sons, 1960.

Locke, John. *Second Treatise of Government*. London: Awnsham Churchill, 1690.

Loutsenhiser, Oliver D. *Packer's Cannibalism*. Montrose, Colorado: (n.p.) 1887.

Macklin, Charles. *Love à la Mode*. Edinborough: Oliver and Boyd, 1759.

Marquard, Ralph L. *Jokes and Anecdotes for All Occasions*. New York: Hart Publishing, 1977.

Maximus, Valerius. *Valerius Maximus, His Collections of Memorable Acts and Sayings, Book six*. London: (n.p.) 1684.

McCall, Samuel Walker. *Thaddeus Stevens*. Boston and New York: Houghton, Mifflin, 1899.

McNamara, M. Frances, comp. *Ragbag of Legal Quotations.* Albany: Matthew Bender, 1960.

Merritt, Dixon Lanier. *Nashville Banner.* Nashville, Tennessee: April 22, 1913.

Napoleon I. *Maxims de Guerre.* Paris: Annelin, 1830.

Parker, John Francis. *"If Elected, I Promise . . . ;" Stories and Gems of Wisdom by and About Politicians.* Garden City, New York: Doubleday, 1960.

Pollock, Milton B. "Some Practical Aspects of Appellate Advocacy," *New York State Bar Bulletin.* Albany: New York State Bar, February 1959.

Proffatt, John. *Curiosities and Law of Wills.* San Francisco: Sumner, Whitney, 1876.

Redden, Kenneth, and Veron, Enid L., comps. *Modern Legal Glossary.* Charlottesville, Virginia: Michie, 1980.

Rees, Nigel. *Quote . . . Unquote.* London and Boston: G. Allen & Unwin, 1978.

Ringo, Miriam, comp. *Nobody Said It Better.* Chicago: Rand McNally, 1980.

Russell, Leonard. *English Wits.* London: Hutchinson, 1940.

Sandburg, Carl. *Complete Poems.* New York: Harcourt, Brace, 1950.

Seitz, D. C. *Whistler Stories.* New York and London: Harper & Brothers, 1913.

Selden, John. *Table-Talk.* London: Printed for
E. Smith, 1689.

Shakespeare, William. *Troilus and Cressida.*
London: G. H. Davidson, 1603.

———. *Merry Wives of Windsor.* London: G. H.
Davidson, 1602.

———. *King Henry VI, Part II.* London: G. H.
Davidson, 1591.

Shaw, George Bernard. *Misalliance.* London:
Constable, 1914.

Sherard, Robert Harborough. *The Life of Oscar
Wilde.* London: T. W. Laurie, 1906.

Shrager, David, and Frost, Elizabeth, eds. *The
Quotable Lawyer.* New England Publishing
Associates, 1986.

Simpkin, et al. *The Majesty of the Law.*
London: Simpkin, Marshall, Hamilton, Kent
& Co. Ltd., 1900.

Stone, Irving. *Clarence Darrow for the Defense.*
Garden City, New York: Doubleday, Doran,
1941.

———. *They Also Ran.* Garden City, New York:
Doubleday, Doran, 1945.

Strong, Theron. *Joseph H. Choate.* New York:
Dodd, Meade, 1917.

Sunday Times. [London]. "Here, the Law Is a
Jungle." December 29, 1985, p. 1, col. E.

Sutherland, James, ed. *The Oxford Book of Literary Anecdotes.* Oxford: Clarendon Press, 1975.

Swift, Jonathan. *A Critical Essay upon the Faculties of the Mind (1707)* in Rawson, Claude, ed. *A Collection of Critical Essays.* Englewood Cliffs, New Jersey: Prentice-Hall, 1995.

Tacitus, various eds. *Annals.* London: Methuen & Co., 1959.

Tarbell, Ida M. *The Life of Elbert Gary.* New York and London: Appleton, 1925.

Tegg, William. *Wills of Their Own.* Self-published, 1876.

Woodward, Robert, and Armstrong, Scott. *The Brethren.* New York: Simon and Schuster, 1979.

Wycherley, William. *The Plain Dealer.* London: T.N., printed for R. Bently and M. Magnes, 1677.

Zall, Paul M., ed. *Abe Lincoln Laughing: Humorous Anecdotes from Original Sources by and about Abraham Lincoln.* Berkeley: University of California Press, 1982.

Index of Names

Adams, Thomas (1807–1874), American clergyman and poet, 167

Ade, George (1866–1944), American humorist and playwright, 166

Bacon, Francis (1561–1626), British lawyer and writer, 176

Bentham, Jeremy (1748–1832), British philosopher, 128, 155

Bierce, Ambrose Gwinnett (1842–1914?), American writer and poet, 171, 175, 177

Brougham, Henry Peter, Baron Brougham and Vaux (1778–1868), British lawyer and statesman, 172

Bryan, William Jennings (1860–1925), American lawyer, orator, and presidential contender, 162

Burns, Robert (1759–1796), Scottish poet, 135, 173

Burton, Harold H. (1888–1964), American jurist, 192

Byron, George Gordon (1788–1824), English poet, 219

Carroll, Lewis (Charles Lutwidge Dodgson) (1832–1898), English writer and mathematician, 201, 218

Choate, Joseph Hodges (1832–1917), American lawyer and diplomat, 163

Clive, Robert, Baron Clive of Plassey (1725–1774), English soldier and statesman, 215

Curran, John Philpot (1750–1817), Irish lawyer and jurist, 181, 196

Darrow, Clarence Seward (1857–1938), American lawyer, 81, 168

Depew, Chauncey Mitchell (1834–1928), American lawyer and politician, 168

Dickens, Charles (1812–1870), English writer, 170

Douglas, William Orville (1898–1980), American jurist, 184

Dunne, Finley Peter (1867–1936), American writer and humorist, 33, 176

East India Company, 215

Ellenborough, Edward Law, 1st Baron (1750–1818), British lawyer and jurist, 48, 181

Erskine, John (1695–1768), Scottish jurist and professor, 167

Fox, Charles James (1749–1806), English politician, 174

France, Anatole (Jacques-Anatole-François Thibault) (1844–1924), French writer and poet, 53

Frost, Robert Lee (1874–1963), American poet, 87, 173

Giraudoux, Jean (1882–1944), French writer and diplomat, 172

Heine, Heinreich (1797–1856), German poet, 139

Herbert, Sir Alan Patrick (1890–1971), British writer and politician, 174

Holmes, Oliver Wendell, Jr. (1841–1935), American jurist, 128

Jerrold, Douglas (1803–1851), English playwright and humorist, 173

Johnson, Samuel (1709–1784), English lexicographer and wit, 165, 218

Jumblatt, Walid (1949–), Lebanese militant, 33

Kipling, Rudyard (1865–1936), English writer and poet, 33

Lamb, Charles (1775–1834), English writer, 165

Locke, John (1632–1704), English philosopher, 34

Lord Douglas (Alfred Bruce) (1870–1945), British poet, 226

Lord Jeffreys, English jurist, 165

Louis XII (1462–1515), French king, 171

Macklin, Charles (1697–1797), Irish actor and playwright, 175

Marshall, John (1755–1835), American jurist, 182

Maynard, Sir John (1602–1690), English lawyer, 165

Mizner, Wilson (1876–1933), American businessman and wit, 227

Morgan, John Pierpont (1837–1913), American financier, 170

Napoleon I (Napoleon Bonaparte) (1769–1821), French general and emperor, 32

Nixon, Richard (1913–1995), American president, 183, 213

Packer, Alferd G. (1830?–1875?), American frontiersman, 6

Rabelais, François (1494?–1553), French writer, 144

Riqueti, Honoré Gabriel, Comte de Mirabeau (1749–1791), French revolutionary statesman, 175

Roosevelt, Theodore (1858–1919), American president, 184

Rowland, Henry Augustus (1848–1901), American physicist and professor, 226

Ruskin, John (1819–1900), British critic and social reformer, 103

Sage, Russell (1816–1906), American financier, 219

Sandburg, Carl (1878–1967), American poet and writer, 167

Shakespeare, William (1564–1616), British playwright and poet, 34, 150, 169

Shaw, George Bernard (1856–1950), Irish playwright, 34

Smith, Frederick Edwin, 1st Earl of Birkenhead (1872–1930), British lawyer and politician, 46, 163, 197

Smith, Sydney (1771–1845), British clergyman and writer, 172

Stevenson, Robert Louis (1850–1894), Scottish writer, 140

Stone, Irving (1903–1989), American writer, 86, 171

Tacitus (c. 56–c. 117), Roman senator and historian, 166

Twain, Mark (Samuel Longhorne Clemens) (1835–1910), American humorist and writer, 76

Vidal, Gore (1925–), American novelist and essayist, 63

Voltaire (François Marie Arouet) (1694–1778), French philosopher, writer, and wit, 220

Whistler, James Abbott McNeill (1834–1903), American-born British artist, 103

Wilde, Oscar Fingal O'Flahertie Wills (1854–1900), British playwright, writer, and wit, 226

Wycherley, William (1640–1716), British playwright, 218